God'sidences

God's Intervention Today

A Faith-Builder Book

This book is designed to build your faith,
as is the goal of all Faith-Builders' books.

Books by Glorian Bonnette

God'sidences (God's Intervention Today)

Prophetic Assignments . . . of the God-kind

God'sidences

God's Intervention Today

Glorian L. Bonnette

Faith-Builders' Publishing
Kent, Washington

God'sidences (God's Intervention Today)

Copyright © 2005 by Glorian L. Bonnette

Faith-Builders' Publishing
P.O. Box 3993, Kent, WA 98089 USA

Email: faithbp@att.net

ISBN 0-9764234-0-5

Cover by Lee Pierce

ALL RIGHTS RESERVED

No part of this publication may be reproduced, stored in a retrieval system, or transmitted in any form or by any means—electronic, mechanical, photocopy, recording, or otherwise—without the express prior permission of Faith-Builders' Publishing, with the exception of brief excerpts in magazine articles and/or reviews.

All inquiries about reprinting and/or translating into other languages should be addressed to Faith-Builders' Publishing.

Printed in the United States of America.

This book is dedicated to

Rusty, Kory, and Holly
&
Stephen, Jaroslaw, and Janifer

SPECIAL THANKS

First and foremost I give thanks to Jesus Christ my Lord Who never fails to surprise, amaze, enable, and delight me. Special thanks also go to: Barry and Carolyn Bowers, Rex and Judy Miller, Paul and Rebecca Stolton, who love and encourage me consistently. To all the men and women of God who have spoken into my life (knowingly and unknowingly), and to all those who have heard the voice of God and supported me in prayer and with finances. To the thousands of brothers and sisters in Christ who kept prompting me to write. To Janifer, SK, Angela, Jo, Bruce and Judy, for believing in the value of this book. To Sarah, who works with God to keep me fit and on the road. To Lee Pierce who formatted this book, and for her patience while designing the front and back covers. Last, but not least, to Annette Bradley, to whom I am most grateful for editing the manuscript and for walking me through the publishing process.

ABOUT THE AUTHOR

After traveling and ministering in 40 plus nations for the past 16 years, Glorian Bonnette, an ordained minister, has observed that the most effective sermons are those which include her personal "stories" . . . in other words, sharing testimonies of God's intervention in her life and in the lives of others. Faith rises wherever she ministers. She believes God for her every provision and is living proof that God can, and does, do what He says He will do!

Affectionately referred to as, "Mama Glo," Glorian preaches in churches of many different doctrinal persuasions, in conferences, Christian gatherings, Bible Schools, leadership meetings, and crusades, as well as appears on television and radio programs nationally and internationally. She also takes teams of various sizes on prophetic assignments, teaching them how to walk by faith as they go.

Glorian has three adult children, seven grandchildren, and one great grandchild. She currently resides in Des Moines, Washington, when she is not traveling.

Her primary focus is to help the Body of Christ grow to maturity and to help those in bondage to religious spirits shake them off and awaken to the truth of God's Word, that they may live by faith in the Son of God, in reality, and not by mere mental assent. Her passion is to witness Christians coming to know God's great love deep in their hearts. Often you will hear her say, **"Dare to believe! What have you got to lose?"**

TABLE OF CONTENTS

Introduction 9

Part One—A Shocking Salvation
The Holy Spirit's Secret 19
Holy Ghost Revelation 23
Life Through New Eyes 27
Normal Christian Living 28
The Mall 29
With a Loud Crash 31
A Pillar of Cloud 32
The First Dream 34
God Brings Them to the Door 36
Sears Department Store 38
Getting My Attention 40
Finding the Church 44
An Offering 47
Training Ground 49

Part Two—Supernatural Healings (Mine and Others)
Front Page News 55
It Disappeared 58
The 700 Club 60
A Lady in Waiting 62
A Hospital Run 64
The Young and the Old Can Come to Jesus 66
Beyond Medical Knowledge 68
A Strange Event (In the old training ground) 70

Part Three—"Words," Visions, and Events

The Toaster Plug Cover 75
The Z28 Camaro 78
The Giving Man 83
Checks, Checks, and More Checks 84
Dreams (Night Visions) 86
Visions (Internal Pictures) 88
Rocks and Rebar 92
Swords Everywhere 94
More Swords 96
Knighted (With an Imaginary Sword) 98
A Flaming Sword 99
The Real Thing 100
A Woman With a Sword 102
Divine Appointments 104
Steps Ordered by God 110
On the Way to Jakarta 113
A Heart for Poland 117
The Hotel Clerk 120
The Pastor 121
Angels Everywhere 123
Our Eyes Were Blinded 128
Prophetic in Number 132
Prophetic Numbers Continued 135
Croatia 138

INTRODUCTION

"For the testimony of Jesus is the spirit of prophecy."
Revelation 19:10b (NKJV)

Jesus Christ **alive and well in you** (testimony) is the spirit of prophecy (declaration). (Rev. 19:10b) Your testimony is not merely what you say. It is **who you are** as you live your life before God and others in honesty and obedience. It is who you are as you let the love of Jesus Christ shine, and as you allow Him to show forth His glory and magnificence through you in the midst of your obedience.

Simply be obedient to the next thing the Lord leads you to do and then the next, and the next . . . before you know it you will understand how every step leads to the next step, progressively bringing you into maturity and the likeness of Christ.

As a quick reference, think about Noah building the ark. It was not what he said that showed forth the soon-coming events. No, it was the act of building the ark in obedience to God. (See the story Genesis, chapters 6-10.)

The Dictionary defines "testimony and testimonial" this way: Testimony—(1) The statement of a witness under oath; (2) Evidence in support of a fact or statement; (3) Open declaration, as of faith. (4) Public declaration regarding some experience.

Testimonial—(1) A written declaration recommending a person or thing; (2) Something given or done as an expression of admiration or gratitude.

God'sidences (God's Intervention Today)

The stories contained within this book are true. Because God intervened, they became powerful testimonies. As you read, my prayers and hopes are that you will grow in faith and dare to believe that you, too, can be about our Father God's business. Trust and obedience are the required substances.

This volume is not intended to be a preaching or teaching text (though I dare say you may gain something from reading it). It is being recorded as the Lord leads and brings to remembrance those supernatural events which I have witnessed.

This is a testimonial, a written declaration of the greatness of Jesus Christ. To Him belongs all honor, all glory and all praise!

GOD'SIDENCE. This is the word that the Lord dropped into my heart years ago to replace the word "coincidence" when used in reference to God and His supernatural intervention into our lives. As you read these pages you will see the word God'sidence written in parentheses after each act of His supernatural intervention that I could recognize. I am sure that there are multiple times the Lord intervenes of which I am unaware, even to this day. Often, after the fact and with 20/20 hindsight, I recognize well His dealings, although I was unaware of it at the time.

PART ONE

A SHOCKING SALVATION

Having hated God and Christians as far back in my life as I could remember, in my way of thinking joining their ranks was not an option. I did not know why I hated God, but at least knew why I hated Christians. As far as I was concerned they were all hypocrites! And the name of Jesus spoken in my presence? Not on your life! (Unless it was a swear word.) I was about as anti-Christ and anti- Christian as one could get and so was my husband. Just to help you better understand, please note that if my children even so much as spoke the name "Jesus," my anger was so aroused that I instantly would begin yelling, "Not in my house you don't!" I was opposed violently to the very name of Jesus.

I do not wish to go into all the ugly details of my fear-filled sordid life prior to knowing Jesus. Just understand and know that life never had been easy for me. Having known lots of physical and sexual abuse from the time of four years old, there were deep wounds within my heart. The ways of thinking and reacting within clouded the ability to make sound decisions during most of my 39 years of life. The only reason I am giving you this much information is so that you can get a realistic picture of the events of which I am about to tell you.

It was the last week of February, 1982. I was in a terrible state of mind. The deep pain inside my heart was almost unbearable. I was once again faced with making a major life-changing decision and did not know which way to turn. My marriage was terrible and I knew I had to do something but did not know what. I felt that no matter which road I ultimately chose to fol-

Part One—A Shocking Salvation

low, it surely would be the wrong one. My track record was not a winning one. Every night for a week I had been getting up after everyone had gone to bed. I was trying to figure out which route to take. This night was no different than the previous seven . . . I thought!

It was around 11:00 p.m. when I left my bed and went into the living room. After walking back and forth in the dark for a bit, I sat down and smoked a cigarette. The battle raging within my mind was exhausting. Emotionally I was on the edge! I felt completely unable to think reasonably, and I had absolutely no idea of what immediately was to follow.

Suddenly, with a surge of energy, I jumped up and began to shake my fists toward the ceiling and scream at God! "God are you real? Do you really have a Son named Jesus? Is He God? If You could prove it to me, I'd follow you!" (GOD'SIDENCE!)

Instantly tears were streaming down my face. (GOD'SIDENCE!)

I had no idea why there were tears or why I just had yelled what I did. I thought I must be "venting" all my anger and tossed emotions.

I went over to my couch and lay down on my back. The tears still were flowing rapidly down both sides of my head and into my ears and hair. I do not know how long I laid there in the dark in that state, but at some point I became aware that my stomach was in great pain. It felt as if it were being ripped apart, as though I were being pulled in two directions at the same time. I suddenly opened my eyes and saw that the living room had filled with light! (GOD'SIDENCE!) Quickly I closed them again because I could not look at the light in the room—it was too bright! I kept trying to peek ever so slightly but could not. This light was more than just light, it was substance . . . or? I do not know how long I laid there that way. It could have

God'sidences (God's Intervention Today)

been moments or hours, I have no time frame, but it seemed an eternity. All I knew was that my stomach hurt and I could not look at the light.

While yet in that state, I next realized that my body was on fire— all over! (GOD'SIDENCE!) There was not a nerve on my body that had not been set aflame. Then I had this thought, "Hum, I must be having another stroke. Hum, I must be having another stroke. Hum, I must be having another stroke." (I had a stroke at the age of 24.) It wasn't a fearful thought, just sing-songy and repetitive. After awhile (who knows how long), I thought to myself, "Glo, you had better get up and get some help." I tried to get up and discovered that I was paralyzed over my entire body. (GOD'SIDENCE!) The only physical portions of my body that were mobile, were my eyelids. Yet, I really couldn't lift them either because, even though they were mobile, the light was too bright to use them.

After awhile, the light began to fade and, as it did my body began returning to normal. There I was lying on my couch in the dark. I sat up for a moment, then stood up and started walking toward the bedroom. About half way there I became aware of the fact that there was a smile on my face. (GOD'SIDENCE!) Not a small little tilt of the mouth, but an ear-to-ear plastered-type smile. I thought to myself, "You're crazy! You are getting ready for another stroke or something and you're smiling about it. You've lost your mind!" I tried to stop smiling but I could not. I even reached up, put my hands to my face, and tried to force the smile off. I know it sounds really strange but that's what happened.

Reaching my bedroom, I crawled into my bed and went right to sleep (that alone was a miracle). The next conscious moment I had, I found myself standing in the dark in my living room. Having never been a sleepwalker, this was very strange,

Part One—A Shocking Salvation

indeed. I remember shaking my head as if to express "What are you doing?" I returned to my bed and went right back to sleep. I believe what was going on is that somehow, at least subconsciously, I was trying to make sense of what had happened earlier.

To make things perfectly clear, never once did the thought occur to me that what had transpired had anything to do with God! I had not understood that what I thought was "venting anger" was a cry from deep within my heart for truth! "If a man searches for God with his whole heart, God is faithful and will prove Himself to that man." (Deut. 4: 29 *NAS*)

The next morning I got up and got ready for work as usual. I was not thinking about the night before. My mind was on the scheduled work for that day. My normal routine was to go to work about an hour later than my husband did. During those days we owned a business that was housed in a large warehouse about a half mile from our home.

When I arrived and entered the building, I saw my husband on the other side of the room. Suddenly, it was as if everything went into slow motion, just as a film running at half speed. His back was turned toward me and he was bent over. I saw his hands double into fists as he straightened up and began turning in my direction. As he started coming toward me, I could see that it was his body, his fists, and his head . . . but the thing looking at me from out of his eyes **was not my husband!** (GOD'SIDENCE!) I also knew in every fiber of my being that when he reached me, he was going to hit me (which was not his normal behavior). From out of those eyes came absolute hatred! In a flash, from what seemed as if out of nowhere, my arm flew up and stretched out toward him, and from my mouth I heard these words loudly spoken: "Stop! I do not have to worry about this anymore! I

God'sidences (God's Intervention Today)

have a new manager in my life, the LORD JESUS CHRIST!" (GOD'SIDENCE!)

My husband stopped in his tracks and snarled "Where the ____ ____ did that come from?" In that instant, I knew and understood what had happened the night before. I knew that God was real! I knew that Jesus was real and He was God! I knew that I had been saved and forgiven. I knew that God somehow was going to heal my heart from the inside and I knew God called me as a preacher. I did not know how I knew those things. What I did know was that no one but God Himself ever could have made me say what I did. He, in fact, had proven Himself to me! He was real! (GOD'SIDENCE!) Fleeing from the building, I got into my car and drove home. As quickly as I could I raced into the house and into my bedroom, where I kneeled beside my bed and began to thank God for saving me. Then I asked Him to please give me patience. I needed it because I had none. I also knew I was going to have to "eat crow or humble pie" as the saying goes. I owed a lot of people apologies, especially my family and Christians to whom I had been less than kind.

At one point in my life, five or six years earlier when living in Oregon, I on occasion had sat outside a church, in my car, drunk. I waited for the people to come out so I could tell them how weak they were. I was filled with so much anger! Yelling at them I cried out, "Don't you people know this crap is nothing more than a crutch?" Little did I know that would set them to praying for me, a whole congregation! (GOD'SIDENCE!)

Years later I ministered several times in that very same church! Isn't it amazing how God can orchestrate the events of our lives, all the while drawing us unto Himself? (GOD'SIDENCE!)

My younger sister had been a Christian for 20 years, and my mother had become a born-again believer five years prior

Part One—A Shocking Salvation

to my salvation. For years the two of them were always on what seemed to be two different sides of the fence, yet both claiming to be Christians. I found it laughable. My sister used to say, "Mom is too zealous." My mother would say, "She'll learn." Just so you know, as I witnessed their behavior, as well as that of other Christians, I felt quite justified in my beliefs about Christianity being ridiculous and full of hypocrites. There were many examples throughout my life to that point. Today as a Christian, I understand that **hearts must go through the process of character change, and on the way appearances can seem pretty messy.**

God is redeeming every attitude deep within our hearts that would stand against Him, attitudes of which we may or may not be aware.

One day when I visited with my sister, she said to me, "I am not preaching, but I just want to say this one thing. I was wrong and Mom was right!" After that I do not remember the length of days or weeks but I noticed that the two of them really were no longer in opposition concerning their Christianity. I did not know what their beliefs were but I could see the difference in their behavior toward each other. I do not remember pondering on their situation or even giving it much of a second thought, other than the fact of noticing they were no longer on opposing sides.

After my salvation, my mother informed me that not only had she been praying for me but that the Lord had informed her that when she and my sister came into agreement that my salvation soon would follow. (GOD'SIDENCE!) All this was occurring and I had no knowledge of it! As a matter of fact, I had forbidden my mother or my sister to speak about "religion" in my presence or to my children. Things had been tense for years concerning the issue.

God'sidences (God's Intervention Today)

Hopefully, you now can understand why I would need great patience. I had a lot of repenting and restitution with which to deal.

To continue, while still kneeling beside my bed the Lord gave me a vision. I knew it was from God. Prior to being a Christian I had experienced evil and just about everything the devil had to throw at me (though I did not know it was the devil) but I never had experienced anything such as that vision. (GOD'SIDENCE!!!)

When I got up from my knees I was shaking all over. After calming down, I called my mother to tell her what had happened to me, that I was saved and that I had experienced a vision. She seemed a little dubious but said she would get me a Bible and have it sent that very day by UPS. I received my first Bible, a *New American Standard*, on the following day. I was so excited! I began to read where my mother had instructed me to read. "Start reading the New Testament first," she had said. So that is what I did. After reading Matthew, Mark, and Luke, I stopped and went back and read them again. It seemed to me that those people in the Bible just kept telling the same stories over and over. I started talking to the Lord about it. "Jesus, I know this is Your book. I know it is the truth. But honestly, it really is boring!" That's the way it went for the first two weeks.

The Holy Spirit's Secret

It was exactly two weeks after salvation when one day I came home from work, made a sandwich, and decided to watch the 12:00 o'clock news while I ate. I went into the living room, switched on the television knob, and sat down. I had not paid any attention to the channel to which it was tuned. When the screen lit up (it was an older set and took a few moments to warm up) immediately there was a man pointing his finger directly at me. He said these EXACT words, "Now remember, the Holy Spirit is a gift from God but it can only be yours by possession IF you receive it!" The TV screen then went blank. (GOD'SIDENCE!)

Once again the tears were flooding down my face uncontrollably as I began crying out to the Lord. "God, please!" I begged. "I want everything you have for me! I want it all! God I don't even know what the Holy Spirit is, so how can I receive the gift of it?" Suddenly this thought came to me, "How do you receive any gift?" (GOD'SIDENCE!) As fast as I had that thought, I saw a picture inside my head. I could see a box wrapped in silver foil paper with pink satin ribbon around it and beautiful pink and white roses mixed with a bow on the top. (GOD'SIDENCE) "Oh! OK, Lord." I reached out and took this imaginary box and set it on my lap. As I did so I was describing it to Jesus, "Lord, this is the most beautiful gift I ever have received! I'm opening it now. Are you watching?"

After having gone through all the motions of unwrapping a gift, I then stuck my hands down into this imaginary box sitting

God'sidences (God's Intervention Today)

on my lap, and with hands cupped, lifted out the content and brought it to my heart. As I did so I stated these words, "Alright, Lord, the gift of the Holy Spirit is mine by possession because I receive it!" (GOD'SIDENCE!) Wiping the tears off my face, I chuckled a little at my own "silliness" and went back to work.

The man on the television was Ben Kinchlow, although at the time I did not know who he was.

As far as I knew not one thing happened as a result of my "silly" little episode. And the man on the television had said nothing about anything being attached to this gift. (By the way, when later I had gone over to the television to turn it off, I noticed it was tuned to a station we did not receive! It was very strange. (Hum. . . . GOD'SIDENCE!)

The only difference I recognized during that week was that the Bible began to come alive to me! "Lord, how did I miss all this? This is not boring at all! Wow!" I did not connect this "new understanding" with the "silly little thing" I had done in front of the television. Nor did I connect the incidence with what began occurring during my sleep. Each night or the next morning my family would say "Mom, what's wrong with you? You must be having bad dreams because you keep talking in your sleep, and we can't understand a thing you're saying!" I had no idea to what they were referring. I apologized for waking them, and I kept telling them that it was not intentional, for I couldn't remember any bad dreams (or good ones either).

This had been going on for almost two weeks, when one night while talking I awoke myself due to the noise. (GOD'SIDENCE!) It sounded so funny, as if a baby were gooing and gawing or some such thing. I thought to myself, "Glo, what in the world is the matter with you? You're too young to be going into your second childhood!" That very thought made me start laughing and then I couldn't stop. (GOD'SIDENCE!)

The Holy Spirit's Secret

My husband made me leave the bedroom. I went into the living room and dissolved upon the floor into a heap of heaving laughter. I laughed so much and so hard that my sides hurt for a week afterward. I never had laughed that way in my entire life! I tried to control myself so the family could sleep and so I could breath but it was impossible! (GOD'SIDENCE!) And for the life of me, I could not think of one thing that was funny enough to be causing so much laughter. About four and one-half hours later the laughter finally stopped. Not once had I thought about God being involved in what was happening. I never had heard that God could or would fill someone with laughter. My thinking concerning the behavior of a Christian was yet one of solemnity, reverence and dignity.

The incident of laughter had transpired on a Wednesday night. By Thursday morning I felt the most urgent need to be baptized in water. (GOD'SIDENCE!) I began calling different churches in our area and not one would agree to baptize me. By the time my parents arrived from Oregon for a visit (the first one after my conversion), I was completely despondent. I felt so defeated. In tears of despair, I explained to my mother that obviously I was not worthy to be baptized. Bless my mother for she said, "Glo, it isn't that urgent, but if you feel it is, then let me see what I can do." She made a few phone calls and had success.

The pastor who had agreed to perform the baptism instructed my mother to have me at the church at 10:00 o'clock the following morning, which was on a Friday. That dear saint of a man and his wife had gotten busy Thursday afternoon and evening and called people from their congregation to meet together at the church the next morning to witness and participate in my baptism. (GOD'SIDENCE!) It was a beautiful ceremony and I am and always will be eternally grateful! I thank the Lord

God'sidences (God's Intervention Today)

that this precious pastor heard the voice of the Holy Spirit and did not refuse to baptize me. Pastor Don Coulter always will be one of my heroes. I thank the Lord for him.

When I look back upon that time, it is a wonder to me that I did not feel prompted in any way to attend "church."

Holy Ghost Revelation

It was so exciting to be visiting with my mom and talking about Jesus on that Friday afternoon following the baptismal service. At one point she looked at me a bit strange and asked, "Have you got the Holy Spirit?" "Oh, yes!" I replied. To this day I do not know if she heard from the Lord or not, but she did not say one more word concerning the subject. I answered correctly according to what I knew, but looking back I realize that she meant something entirely different than what was my understanding of having the Holy Spirit.

It was such a wonderful weekend. I was thrilled because for the first time in the history of our family, we all were going to go to church together come Sunday. We had to get up early that morning because our drive was about 100 miles to meet with my sister and her family. The plan was to attend my sister's "new church." Believe me this was an event! My mom and dad (the man who adopted me and my two siblings when I was 14), my sister and her family, my brother and his family, and me and my family all went together. There were 16 of us meeting. The only one missing was the very youngest brother (who became our brother when we were adopted). What a miracle! My sister warned us that we needed to be early if we wanted to sit together because the church was big; about 2,500 or more people attended at that time.

As instructed, we arrived early, and all the men in the family staked out a row very near the back. (The church was holding their Sunday meetings in a school gymnasium, and our row

God'sidences (God's Intervention Today)

was on the floor, not in the bleachers.) We were early enough that the equipment was still in the process of being set up for the service. All 16 of us were waiting quietly as the place began to fill. Suddenly, with no warning, a young red-headed man took a flying leap up onto the stage, grabbed a microphone, and shouted, "Is there anyone in this place who wants the baptism of the Holy Ghost?" (GOD'SIDENCE!) Before I knew what happened, I jumped to my feet and yelled, "I do!" "Then get down here right now!" he yelled. I started to scramble past the members of my family seated to my left. As I did so, they made disparaging comments, "Sit down! You're making a fool of yourself." I did not care if I made a fool of myself! Reaching the aisle, I started running toward the platform, all the while talking to God. "OK, God, I know You are real and I know I am water baptized, and I know I've got the gift of the Holy Spirit, but what the heck is the Holy Ghost?" I really didn't know that the Holy Spirit and the Holy Ghost were the same thing! And I already was water baptized! I did not know what that man was talking about but whatever it was, if it pertained to God, I wanted it! It was almost as if I were being driven toward God. Knowing Him became the most important thing in my life. (GOD'SIDENCE!)

When I reached the front, the young preacher pointed to a lady sitting nearby in the front row and told her to take me into one of the side rooms and get me filled with the Holy Ghost. Away we went. As we settled in a room, she began to read Scripture from the Bible about the infilling of the Holy Spirit and the gift of speaking in tongues.

I was stunned! A strange feeling began to come over me, and as I looked at her, I stated, "Excuse me, please, I know that the Bible is true. But this 'tongues thing' is not for me." She had the most mischievous, knowing kind of expression on her face

Holy Ghost Revelation

as she said to me, "Oh, Sweetie, just raise your hands and say, 'Hallelujah.'" (GOD'SIDENCE!) I felt so awkward and embarrassed as I sat trying to explain that I did not mean to be rude, but . . . . Again she repeated, "Come on, just raise your hands and say, 'Hallelujah.' You can do it!" I remember thinking to myself that if I just hurried and did what she asked, I could get out of there. I decided to "just do it," but then my arms became heavy and felt as lead weights as I tried to raise them. Shaking, I finally succeeded in raising them, and as I started to say "Hallelujah," something different came rushing out of my mouth. (GOD'SIDENCE!) Instantly, with the shock of the whole thing, I jumped up and said, "I can't do this!" and began running out of the room. In order to get to the outside of the building, I first had to pass in front of the entire assembly. I did not care, I just wanted out! As soon as I hit the outdoors and was in the parking lot, I threw my arms into the air and started speaking (loudly) in the most incredible utterance from some language I knew not! All I knew was that it was God!

It was such a shock to me. The truth is, as soon as I had heard the very first sounds come out of my mouth, back inside that room with that dear sister, I had understanding of what had been happening in my sleep at night for the previous two weeks. (GOD'SIDENCE!) What a strange mixture of emotions erupted from within me. Perhaps it was the embarrassment I felt in front of her, or maybe I was just so overwhelmed by everything that I needed to be able to do this thing alone with God. It all happened so fast. Once I began speaking in tongues, though, I did not stop for over 20 hours! I could not stop! I did not want to stop! It was as if experiencing freedom after having been in prison my whole life. I was so excited!

When the family members came outside after service and began to ask questions, I only answered them in tongues. I do not know what they thought, because they just began to shake their heads and walk away, acting embarrassed. It was the last week of March, 1982, one month from the date of my salvation. (I find it interesting that I was two weeks away from my 39th birthday when I got saved. Then I got the gift of the Holy Spirit on my 39th birthday. Thirty-nine are the numbers of stripes Jesus took for our healing. GOD'SIDENCE!)

God is the God of supernatural experiences. He can deal with a person in any way He chooses. Not once did I say the "sinners" prayer, yet I was saved. I was baptized in the Holy Spirit without even knowing what it was, plus it happened prior to water baptism. GOD LOOKS AT THE HEART!

Life Through New Eyes!

I was so happy being a Christian. Of course, I continued to do my daily chores at work and at home, but my routine had changed somewhat. Instead of working at a normal pace, I was hurrying to be finished so I could read the Word. I would rush home and grab my bottle of booze and my cigarettes, then race to my bedroom so I could be alone with God and with His Word. I began to consume the Bible! (GOD'SIDENCE!)

The first major change I noticed concerning my behavior was that I wasn't swearing anymore. I did not try to stop. God just caused my speech patterns to change. (GOD'SIDENCE!) Prior to salvation, my mouth was like a sewer. Obscenities were a part of my everyday language. After salvation, they weren't! In the natural, that would have been an impossible task to undertake, but suddenly I no longer was even tempted to swear. God is mighty!

Normal Christian Living

As I read the Word of God, my thoughts were being challenged constantly. I remember reading Mark chapter 16 verse 15: "Go into all the world and preach the gospel to every creature." The words hit me like lightning. (GOD'SIDENCE!) I was created to be a preacher, therefore, I was supposed to be preaching! God was telling me to go out there and tell people about Jesus! That very hour, having been compelled by the Holy Spirit, I went to the streets of our local city in the downtown area and began to tell people about Jesus. Stopping them on the sidewalk, I would say to them, "Please stop for just a minute and let me tell you what has happened to me! I don't really know much about the Bible yet, but I know Jesus is real! I know He is real because He has changed my life!" I would go on tell them the events that had transpired in the recent weeks and months. Here is the strange part about all this . . . PEOPLE WERE GETTING SAVED! (GOD'SIDENCE!) I couldn't answer their questions biblically, but I could talk to God on their behalf right then and there and then lead them into a prayer of seeking Him as the One Who would intervene and change their lives, too!

I did not think this behavior was strange. I thought it was normal Christian behavior. After all, that's what the Bible told us to do. (**Obedience** is better than sacrifice and **is worship unto God!**)

The Mall

My heart's desire was to be obedient to whatever Jesus asked of me. I remember one of the first "assignments" He gave me. I had been saved for several months when one morning He whispered this to me: "Glorian, go to the mall." Please understand that prior to salvation these kinds of things or thoughts never had occurred to me. I recognized them as the voice of God!

Wanting to be obedient to the Lord, I drove to the mall. After I arrived and went inside, I realized I did not know what to do. I stood for a few moments and then asked the Lord what He wanted me to do. "Sing," was His reply. Instantly I was embarrassed and scared. This was new territory, and although I did not want to be disobedient, at the same time I did not want to appear deranged. At that moment I felt as if I were the weakest person alive. I begged God to help me and give me the courage to do what He asked of me.

As I stood there in the mall, I surveyed the hallway and located an area of indentation. It was there that the assignment was accomplished. I tucked myself into that corner, crossed one arm over the front of my body, and rested the elbow of the other arm upon it so I could make a fist and somewhat cover my mouth with it. Then very quietly (almost under my breath) I sang, "Jesus loves me, this I know, for the Bible tells me so," etc. It was the only Christian song I knew or at least could remember that I knew. Quickly I finished the song, and then immediately left the building, returned to my car, and drove

God'sidences (God's Intervention Today)

home. I was positive that absolutely no one could have heard me and my reputation was fully in tact.

I was so excited to know that, indeed, God had strengthened me enough (given His grace) actually to complete the "assignment" He had given me. (GOD'SIDENCE!) However, I must admit, I did not know what He expected to accomplish through it. (I since have understood that it was me He was training.)

The very next day I received an irate telephone call from a family member. "How dare you embarrass our family this way! How could you?" I was stunned, "What on earth are you talking about?" "I'm talking about you standing up on a bench in the mall and singing at the top of your lungs!" I tried to tell her that was not what I had done but she couldn't hear me and hung up.

That was one of the first times I realized that God could take the smallest bit of obedience and magnify it beyond our thinking or understanding. (GOD'SIDENCE!) Realization came immediately, because the fact was that unless someone had stood very close to me and actually leaned in, they could not possibly have heard me in the natural. **What God did was in the supernatural!** (Of course, the part about standing on a bench etc., is just the way gossip goes and grows.)

I started to notice that things for which I prayed began to happen. Then the very thoughts I would think began to happen, as if I had prayed. I actually became somewhat frightened during that time, being concerned that perhaps I might pray or think something "wrong". Childish thinking I know, but in seeing the connection, I became more cautious concerning what I laid before the Lord. After all, perhaps the Lord did not want the things I wanted or perhaps He wanted them at a different time, I reasoned. **The Holy Spirit was teaching me.**

With a Loud Crash!

Strange things began to happen that I could not ignore. I remember coming to the Lord one day very upset because the night before I had tried my best (unsuccessfully) to get my husband away from the TV set. I wanted to have a conversation with him but he was so engrossed in the television that I could not tear him away. "God, can't you help me? I hate that stupid squawk box! I wish it would just quit!" Immediately there was a loud ripping, tearing noise. All I could think of was that our house had been hit by something. I ran outside to see what just had happened. What a shock! The television antenna (which was very huge) had just doubled over (bent in half) and fallen from the chimney where it had been secured. There was no natural explanation! (GOD'SIDENCE!)

A Pillar of Cloud

Another time during that first year, I was attending a conference with my mother, held at the Seattle Center (the old World's Fair grounds where the famous Space Needle sits). The speaker was Kenneth Hagin, Sr.

To get an accurate picture of what was transpiring within me, you need to know that I was an avid smoker! Four packs a day for 20 years. Addicted to the max (which is an understatement).

That building is enormous in size, and my Mother had secured seats for us in the third row from the front, on the floor level, nearest to the stage. I was having a very difficult time sitting there because I wanted a cigarette in the worst way. I told my Mother that I was going to go out and have one. She grabbed my arm and said, "Just sit still. If you don't, you'll miss something!" I sat in agony for possibly another five minutes before I happened to turn sideways and spot a cloud of smoke. (GOD'SIDENCE!) I leaned over to my Mother and said, "Look at that Mom, someone is smoking right here inside the building!" "Where?" my Mother asked. I tried to direct her so she could see it but was unsuccessful. "Mom, how could you not see that?" I watched as that cloud of smoke wafted past us at the end of our row and just kept moving on toward the stage. Just as the "cloud of smoke" hit the platform, Rev. Hagin said, "Folks, the Holy Spirit is here in manifi. . . ." (GOD'SIDENCE!) That was the end of Rev. Hagin speaking that night. That cloud reached him and he fell over. There he was, lying flat on his

A Pillar of Cloud

back on the stage. I thought he had fainted or had a heart attack and needed help! No one seemed to be bothered by Rev. Hagin's fall except me.

Everything happened so fast, and I had no concept of what was going on spiritually. I really believed someone was smoking and the cloud of smoke hit the speaker. It never dawned on me that in the natural a puff (or even many puffs) of smoke from a cigarette could not have continued to stay in a cloud form. (GOD'SIDENCE!) In the natural, it would have dissipated. Again, my Mother grabbed my arm, rather forcefully, and said, "You just saw the Holy Spirit!" Her eyes were wide and she appeared shocked. I did not know what to think of what she just had said. I still was convinced that someone was smoking. "No, Mom. It was just smoke!" It was not until later that I understood what I had witnessed. When I read the account of God leading the children of Israel with a "pillar of cloud by day" and a "pillar of smoke by night," I understood in actuality how that was possible. (Exodus 13: 21)

The First Dream

I had been walking with the Lord for about 16 - 17 weeks when I began having thoughts that perhaps I was crazy! Maybe my husband was right and I was suffering under some kind of delusion. Maybe this whole thing with Jesus wasn't real. At the time I did not realize that these thoughts were coming from the devil, the enemy of my soul. I continued to talk with God, though, "Am I crazy? Have I just made all this up? What's wrong with me?".

Shortly thereafter I had a dream one night. (GOD'SIDENCE!) In this dream I entered into and saw the inside of a small church. I was viewing it as though I had entered from the back of the sanctuary and was walking toward the front, down the center aisle. I remember looking at both sides of the room; each side had several windows, all of which were draped in a heavy red fabric. I stopped about halfway to the front and was watching two men at the podium. They were playing a game . . . Paper, Scissors, or Rock.

This is a hand game played by two people. Each person holds one hand out flat while the other hand is folded into a fist. Then they hit the flat hand with the fisted hand and begin counting. On the third count, the position of the fisted hand is changed to represent paper, scissors, or a rock. It was 14 years before the Lord showed me what that part of the dream meant. (GOD'SIDENCE!)

While watching those men (in the dream), my Mother came up behind me and put her hand on my shoulder, saying,

The First Dream

"Come. I have someone I want you to meet." I turned around and followed my Mother to the back of the room where one wooden pew was facing backward. Sitting on the pew was a little old man and a little old woman. They both were dressed in their Sunday best. The little man had on a dark suit and tie, and the little lady had on a crimson-colored suit with a pillbox hat to match. My Mother started to introduce me to them when they interrupted her and said, "Oh, but we would like to introduce you to . . . " and they held out their hands toward a table. As I turned in the direction to which they were pointing, I saw a table but proclaimed, "Oh, a lampstand!" In my dream "lampstand" was the word that registered to describe the slender round table I saw. It was approximately three feet high and had three ornate curved wrought iron legs. The top of the table and the shelf located mid-way down both were made of marble. I looked at the "lampstand" puzzled, but then a ball of light began to glow about two-and- one half feet above the table. The light continued to grow brighter and in the midst of it a face began to materialize. The face stayed fuzzy in appearance but the eyes became clear and were looking directly into mine. I wanted to dive or melt into those eyes. They were as pools of liquid love. I do not know how to explain it any better. It was at that point in the dream I awoke, and sat up in the bed, saying out loud, "You're real! You are really real! Jesus You're really real! Thank You, thank You, thank You." (GOD'SIDENCE!) Tears of joy clouded my ability to focus clearly as I turned on the bedside light and scrambled for a piece of paper on which to record the dream. I don't know why I bothered because I've never forgotten it.

That dream so established in my heart the reality of Jesus that I never have questioned His existence since. (GOD'SIDENCE!)

God Brings Them to the Door

As the year progressed many were the "strange happenings" (GOD'SIDENCES!). For instance, one day I had the distinct impression that I was to tell someone about Jesus. For some reason I could not go to town that day and told the Lord I was sorry. (Town was the only place that came to mind because I already had told all my neighbors.) A little later in the day there was a knock on my front door. When I opened it, there stood a man looking incredibly confused and misplaced or lost. I asked him if I could help him. His stuttering reply was, "I - I - I don't know why I'm here! I was just driving south on the freeway from Vancouver (BC) and I just turned off and drove here. I don't know why!" (GOD'SIDENCE!) By the time that gentleman had finished making his statement, the Holy Spirit had nudged me and I knew why he was there. "Come on in, I know why you're here." God is so gracious that when I could not go out, He brought someone in. That day God gave me the wonderful privilege of sharing Jesus with that precious man and leading him through a prayer for salvation. That same kind of incident happened twice that year. The second time it was a lady. (GOD'SIDENCE!)

Stop for just a moment and think about what God was doing. He was leading both of those people in ways they did not understand or know, even though they were not yet Christians. **God had a plan!** Continually God proved Himself big! (and still does). I came to see that He could do anything He chose to do. My neighbors, who all joked and teased me about "getting

God Brings Them to the Door

religion," actually were watching the things that were going on at our house. They witnessed the major changes in me. Though most of them would not have admitted it at the time, God was touching them. It wasn't long before some of them would come or call secretly to tell me about a relative or someone in the neighborhood that needed prayer. They were not just "gossiping," they had genuine concern, but they did not feel that God would listen to them. Little did they know at that time that it was the Lord tugging on their hearts with His compassion! (GOD'SIDENCE!)

Sears Department Store

Another time during that year, while simply cleaning the house, I had the very distinct thought, "Go to Sear's!" It came from out of the blue. (GOD'SIDENCE!) I had not been thinking about God, nor had I been praying, but that thought was so strong that I believed it was God. "Okay, Father."

Getting into the car, I drove to the Sear's Department Store, parked, and went inside. I had no idea what the reason was for my being there. I must have appeared a bit strange just standing there, because one of the sales ladies approached and asked me if I were all right. After assuring her that I was fine, I thought perhaps it would be best if I at least appeared to be shopping. While doing so, I tried my best to get an answer from Jesus as to why I was there, but no communication seemed forthcoming.

After being in there for some time I did see something we could use at home. I no longer remember what it was because it was nothing of great importance. When I went to the checkout counter the line was long. I stood there for about five minutes, when all of a sudden the lady in front of me turned around and began telling me she recently had been diagnosed with cancer. She dissolved into tears and then fell into my arms, right there in front of everyone. (GOD'SIDENCE!) As I held her, I didn't know how to comfort her but I did know that Jesus was the only One Who could really help her. "Please, listen to me. Jesus loves you and He is the only One Who can really help! He has the answer."

Sears Department Store

At that point I was so involved in wanting her to hear what I was trying to tell her that I began addressing the other people in the line, as well. "That's right, isn't it?" The other people in line began verbally to agree with me. "That's right, she's telling the truth." Something happened in those ten minutes that can only be described as supernatural intervention. I do not know how to adequately explain what transpired, but it was a time when a group of total strangers united and bonded in agreement and prayer. It was not natural. It was the Divine Hand of God! (GOD'SIDENCE!) I left Sears that afternoon in awe of the mighty workings of the Lord.

Please do not get the idea that everyday there was some major thing happening such as the aforementioned events. I was living a normal everyday existence, with a few exceptions.

The real differences were, the changes in my attitudes. Everyday was a new day! I was so wrapped up in learning about Jesus and His Word that I no longer was dwelling on the problems that were before me prior to salvation. It was as if I had a new lease on life! To me that was a miracle. It was not that the same problems no longer existed. It was simply that I was so busy focusing on Jesus I did not have time to focus on the problems. Besides, when I began to see what God could do, I believed all things were possible. I was in love . . . in love with Jesus!

Getting My Attention

Christmas in 1982 was not the same event it had been in the years previous. Gifts were not so important and I did not feel the same pressures as in the years prior. I mention it because it was then that I received a *Young's Analytical Concordance*. It was a Christmas present from my Mother. I remember looking at it and being completely overwhelmed. How was I ever going to learn all that? (I never will.) For a time, I just set it aside. It just seemed too complicated to tackle until I could have some quiet time.

January came and went but a stirring had begun inside me. I was beginning to feel restless but had no idea why.

One day in February, I was supposed to go to Seattle (about 85 or 90 miles south). I had a business appointment that day. It was cold out and the roads were a bit icy, so I decided to take off early just in case I had to go slow. I went out to the car and tried to start it. Dead! (GOD'SIDENCE!) I went back into the house and got my husband to go out and look at it. While I was waiting, I sat down near the bookcase and happened to spy the Concordance. (GOD'SIDENCE!) Taking it out of its place on the shelf, I placed it upon my lap and opened it to the first page. I started reading the explanations on how to use it. Then there was an example given using the parable of the Talents (Matt. 25:14-30). I read the Scriptures, and just when I had completed the reading, my husband came in and said the car was ready. (GOD'SIDENCE!)

It was a beautiful crisp winter day as I drove down the freeway. Just outside our valley, I decided to turn on the radio and

Getting My Attention

listen to some music. (GOD'SIDENCE!) I turned the knob and came upon a Christian song I recognized. "What a friend we have in Jesus." I was enjoying the music thoroughly, but after a couple of songs an announcement was made. "Today's lesson is from the Book of Matthew, chapter 25." The same parable I just had read 20 minutes earlier. (GOD'SIDENCE!) I thought that was very interesting and funny. I listened for a little bit and then lost the station. Reaching over to the knob I began to try to find another station, this time tuning into one that had a rather jazzy beat. Pretty soon, though, I recognized that it was a medley of Christian songs. I was quite pleased and liked the tempo. When the music stopped, a man began to talk and said, "Our text from the Bible this morning is from the parable of the Talents." (GOD'SIDENCE!) I thought that was really strange! Again the station faded out as I got nearer to Seattle. Once again I was switching channels and again I caught it just in time to hear the speaker say, "Today Dr. 'So & so' is teaching on the parable of the talents." (GOD'SIDENCE!) Whoa! This is a bit too much! It finally hit me that God was trying to get my attention!

(I believe this was about the time I started recognizing there were no coincidences, only God's-incidents.) Already that day the Lord had caused me to read or hear that parable four times! I was excited but did not have the time really to sit and think about what God may be trying to tell me.

When I reached my destination and had registered with the receptionist, I sat down. I looked around for something to read but found nothing. I opened my purse to get a mint or something and started clearing out a few small pieces of paper. As I crossed the room to deposit them into the trash bin, I noticed a sheet of crumpled up paper behind it. Obviously, someone had tried throwing it into the bin and missed. I reached down to

God'sidences (God's Intervention Today)

pick it up off the floor and deposit it in the garbage receptacle. When I did, I happened to see the word "talents." I opened the sheet of paper and would you believe it? THE PARABLE OF THE TALENTS WAS TYPED ON THAT SHEET OF PAPER! (GOD'SIDENCE!) I was shaken visibly! There was absolutely no way this could not be God! I really realized that God was trying to get my attention . . . that it was Him talking to me.

Please note, though, that just because I recognized it was God did not mean that I understood what He was saying to me. There are several good applications that can be attributed to that portion of Scripture.

There is something I would like to address before proceeding. Here it is. **How much or how badly do you want to follow God? To the same degree that you are willing to do anything He asks of you, regardless of your embarrassment or fear of what others will think, is the degree that He proves Himself to you!** Come on, what do you really have to lose by acting upon that which He asks of you? Some **pride** perhaps? Ouch, I know that may sting a little, but really isn't that what we all want deep in our hearts anyway? To die to our pride and allow Him to bring us to the place of humility?

Not everyone is going to be asked to do the same things that the Lord has asked of me. Your task or assignment may be far greater or far less in its entirety but no task is without importance!

I remember a story I heard one time. I don't remember the name of either gentlemen involved but the older of the two had been instructed by the Lord to go to a particular small town in the midwestern part of the United States. I believe the period was the early 1900's. Once there, the Lord told him to preach. So the man secured and set up for meetings in the local schoolhouse. He set about making notices concerning the meetings and then posted them all over town. When the appointed time for the services had rolled around, the man waited and waited but no one ever came.

Being disappointed, he began to inquire of the Lord concerning the matter. The Lord spoke to him and told him to get up and preach. So the man got up and preached! He preached from his heart with fervor, as though there were people in attendance. He did the same thing every night for a week.

For years the whole incident had puzzled him, until one evening when he was attending a meeting where the speaker was a well- known evangelist. It was then that he learned what the Lord had done.

During the evening the well-known minister decided to share his story of salvation. Seems that at one time he was a "railroad tramp" who lived jumping on one train after another. He went on to tell how there was a time when he was in the midwestern part of the United States, and because it was chilly out he had located a schoolhouse and crawled under it to protect himself from the weather. Every evening for a week he laid under that school house and listened to a sermon being preached. He said that he was so convicted that he gave his heart to Jesus!

See? **No task is without importance. Obedience is greater than sacrifice. You do not know what the Lord is about accomplish when He has asked you to do something.** I am sure that gentleman felt foolish but nonetheless he was obedient.

Finding the Church

It was shortly after the incident concerning the parable of the Talents that God began dealing with my heart about going to church. At that point I had been walking with the Lord for a year. When I read the Scripture where we are told not to forsake the gathering together of ourselves, that did it. (Hebrews 10: 25) "Okay, Lord, I'll go!"

Instantly the memory of that dream, about walking into a small church where the windows were draped in red and the "lampstand" experience had transpired, came back to me. (GOD'SIDENCE!) I knew all that I had to do was find that church! It never even occurred to me that I wouldn't. It also never crossed my mind that I could look for it on any day of the week.

So on Sundays I started driving to all the different churches in our county. Upon arrival at each church on my list, I would walk inside and take a look around, never intending to be rude to anyone by stating, "Nope, I'm sorry this isn't the right one." It took me a few weeks to find it, but I did . . . the very same church of my dream! The only difference that I could note was that there was no pew in the back, facing the rear. Plus the little old man and woman never were to appear.

After getting over my initial shock at the rowdiness the first few times I went to church, I loved it. I know I was a handful for my precious pastor because nothing in the church seemed to fit my preconceived ideas of how church should be. I thank the Lord always for sending me where He did. He knew exactly

Finding the Church

what sets of circumstances in which to put me in order to work on my heart.

I also must remind you that in most cases of the God'sidences that occur around me, I'm as surprised as everyone else is. Not surprised that He is doing something, but surprised at what He does and how He does it. It is always similar to being involved in and watching a mystery unfold. (I love mysteries!) To this day I've never gotten over the excitement of God intervening in our lives!

Do I expect Him to intervene? Absolutely! Does He have to do it on my timetable? Absolutely not! Does He have to do it in any pre- prescribed manner? **No!**

Before I continue, let me make this statement: EACH STEP OF OBEDIENCE TO DO WHAT THE LORD ASKS OF YOU ALWAYS WILL LEAD TO THE NEXT STEP! Visualize being at the bottom of a tall staircase . . . you cannot get to the top in one step! No. You must take each step one at a time. As you take each step and you see the result and His enabling power, your faith grows. In essence, you are building a track record with God. For those of you reading this book who would say you don't hear God tell you to do anything, I would encourage you to read the Word (the Bible) . . . even if it is only one chapter a day. If, for instance, you read "forgive" and your heart was pricked, you just heard from God. It is easier to recognize the voice of God if you understand His nature.

Worshiping God through obedience is not a "method" nor is it a set of "rules." It is important for whatever you believe the Lord has asked you to do, that you know how to judge it according to His Word, the Bible. Jesus Christ is Truth! Every Word written in the Bible is for our edification and training in righteousness. The Bible shows forth God's character and His nature.

God'sidences (God's Intervention Today)

It is true that there may be many things that the Lord pricks your heart to do that has not been spoken specifically in His Word, but if it is from God it still must **be as God is.**
Let me give you some examples.
"Stop smoking!" The Bible never mentions anything about cigarettes but it does say, "We are the temple of the Holy Spirit" and should take care of our bodies. Smoking is not healthy. So to hear the Lord say "Stop smoking" agrees with His desire for us to be healthy.
"Go see Uncle Albert." No, the Bible did not mention Uncle Albert but it does mention many times when God sent His own to go see "so & so." So of course, going to see Uncle Albert agrees with the Word. It is the Lord's nature.
"Change lanes, NOW!" "Get off the freeway!" No, there were no freeways mentioned in the Bible but the Lord does warn His people to go a different route or to a different city.

An Offering

One of the first things I can remember that God asked of me after beginning to attend church concerned an offering. For several weeks I had been giving my all, until finally I reached the place where I had given all the money I had available and then all my jewelry. At church one Sunday morning, the offering plea was made and I felt very bad because I had nothing to give to God. As I stood there trying to tell the Lord how sorry I was, this thought came to me; "You have your shoes." (GOD'SIDENCE!) It was a lovely early summer morning and I felt so "dressed." Those lovely blue high heels matched that dress so perfectly. It was one of my favorite outfits, especially when the weather was warm. As I stood there, I went through a complete range of emotions . . . everything from fear of what people might think, to selfishness. I liked my shoes!

My daughter (who was an adult) was with me that morning and out of the blue she grabbed my hand and said, "God would not tell you to do anything that would embarrass me, Mom!"

(GOD'SIDENCE!)

Though I was wrestling with the thought, I am sure no one could have known (unless God revealed it to them) because it was all inside my head. As soon as she spoke, though, I realized it really was God speaking to me.

My desire would be never to embarrass anyone, especially one of my children. So I waited until the offering bucket went by and then slipped out of my seat, went to the back, and quietly deposited my shoes in the offering bucket. The deed was

God'sidences (God's Intervention Today)

done. No use crying over blue shoes! It was actually pretty easy to forget about them through the rest of the service. Many ladies, including myself, often took their shoes off during a service. Even my daughter did not make comment.

After the service, when people were all mulling around talking and laughing, one of the ushers came over to me and whispered that the pastor would like to see me for a moment. I excused myself from the group and went to where the pastor was standing. He was holding his hands behind his back as he said to me, "I want you to know that your gift already has borne fruit." I had no inkling about what he was talking, but right then he brought his hands to the front and gave me back my shoes. He said, "Someone retrieved these in the amount of $10.00." I was so excited I jumped up and down crying, "It really was God. It was Him!" (GOD'SIDENCE!) To top it off, that gift kept bearing fruit for six months. How? The Lord supplied me with offering money for every service. IN FACT THAT WAS THE BEGINNING OF EXPERIENCING GOD'S SUPERNATURAL SUPPLY!

Training Ground

The first "job" the pastor asked me to do was clean the building. He called it the Cleaning Department. Then shortly thereafter, he began a series of sermons about department heads and their responsibilities. Well, after listening to him preach about it, I felt as if there were much I needed to be doing.

If I were a "Department Head," than I needed to be obedient to what the pastor said we were to be doing. In other words, with the help of Jesus, I set about soliciting workers to clean with me. Having managed to get about 20 people and making schedules, etc., we set out to do what the pastor had said Department Heads and department workers were supposed to be doing. "You Department Heads need to be in touch with your people every week. You need to be praying for them and with them and laying hands on them." (GOD'SIDENCE!)

We became a very close group. We viewed cleaning the church rather as being secret agents of God! We started praying over the chairs every service, over the toilets, the podium, and the doors! Then we would be excited watching what was happening during the services. Sometimes we were impressed to pray something specific over a particular area of the seating. Later during the service, the minister (pastor or visiting minister) would do or say something that involved that area specifically, and it would be along the same lines that our department members had prayed. (GOD'SIDENCES!) It was exciting! We actually saw and learned the validity of prayer preparation.

God'sidences (God's Intervention Today)

Next the pastor asked me to teach a Sunday school class, ages three through seven. I was shocked because I did not think I knew enough to teach a class, even to children. After all, I had been in church only about four months. I asked for teaching material but they gave me none, explaining they had not yet decided which courses to order. (GOD'SIDENCE!) I am not complaining because, believe me, it was all the hand of God! So not knowing what to teach, I simply started with Gen. 1:1. I never got out of the first chapter.

After a few weeks, the pastor and his wife approached me asking, "What are you doing in there with all those children? Our son Corey can't wait to get to Sunday morning services so he can be in there!" They went on to say that whatever I was doing it was working great!

To be honest, the children were most often teaching me by asking questions that I had to answer. (GOD'SIDENCE!) Of course, then I believed I had another "Department," and so before class was over we all prayed together. If you don't think you have diversity with children between the ages of three through seven, you need to think again. They are amazing when allowed to speak from their hearts! Our prayer times together were serious! We laid hands on one another and prayed for parents, grandparents, teachers, neighbors, and "boo boos." Many times I left that room in tears. The things for which those little ones would ask God often were heart wrenching. I remember one little tyke asking for prayer for his mommy and daddy because "My daddy gets mad and hits my mommy."

Do you think I was placed in with those children coincidentally? I think not! (GOD'SIDENCE!) While helping them, they were helping me.

About six months into the first year at the church (while still cleaning and still teaching little ones), we had a series of meetings that lasted a couple of weeks. There were a few of the ladies in the congregation who always helped at the altar at the end of the services. They would pass out tissues to people crying and with a large cloth they would cover those, who would "fall down in the spirit" when receiving prayer. It was all so exciting to me. But one night one of the ladies said, "Here, Glo, you do it!" From that point on, none of the ladies would get up to help. It simply became my job. Even when I asked others to do it, they would say "No!" (GOD'SIDENCE!)

I was always embarrassed to be the one in front, but even if I sat and did not go forward to help, no one else did either. I found that I felt responsible for it. It became my "job" for two years! Then the pastor asked me if I would train others to do what I did . . . in other words, make a department. Co-incidence? No-way! (GOD'SIDENCE!)

The Lord used that time of working at the altar to start teaching me to trust what I heard. I was learning the power of the prophetic. Let me give you an example. One time, early on, the visiting minister gave an altar call for healing. About 60 or more people responded. He started on one end and progressively worked through the line, with me following behind him. Nothing unusual had transpired, but when we were praying for about the seventh person, I happened to look down the line, saw a man I never had seen before, and had this thought: "If you would forgive your father your back wouldn't hurt." Instantly I was ashamed of myself for thinking such a thing. I didn't even know this man, let alone for what he was asking prayer. Very quietly I was telling the Lord I was so sorry for thinking judgmental thoughts such as that.

After awhile, we reached the spot where that man stood. The preacher asked him for what he needed prayer, and the man put his hand on his back and said he had terrible back

God'sidences (God's Intervention Today)

pain. Instead of praying right away, the preacher just stood quietly for a moment, then he spoke saying: "The Lord tells me that if you would forgive your father, your back would not hurt anymore." You could have knocked me over with a feather! It was God all the time! (GOD'SIDENCE!)

I started paying closer attention to the thoughts that came while at the altar. After awhile I wanted to test the words for myself. I actually began to speak out prophetically. Scared? Certainly I was! But God was faithful in progressively teaching me. I am telling you truth, sometimes the smallest word spoken sets off a chain reaction that can become a major event! Using a tiny little seed of faith can bring down a mountain.

At one point during this altar-training time, I remember asking the Lord, "What if I make a mistake? What if I'm wrong?" I distinctly heard the Lord say, "Well what if?" It was at that point that I came to the understanding that if we—those called by His name—make a mistake, it would not be the end of the world. God is bigger than our mistakes and He can fix it if we do make a mistake!

I began to understand that **THE LORD ALWAYS LOOKS AT THE INTENT OF THE HEART!** He honors the intention, when carried out in the light of wanting to be obedient to Him, because you love Him and you want to honor Him.

I know what some of you reading this are thinking, right this minute, things such as, "Yeah that's OK for you but I don't hear God that way." Sure you do! You simply may not believe it's God! I find that new Christians (sometimes old ones, too), are afraid to act upon the thought that comes (God's voice), because they are concerned that they "might be wrong." Then there is also the concern that if they were wrong, **they would look bad. PLEASE LISTEN. YOU NEVER WILL KNOW UNTIL YOU ACT UPON IT WHETHER OR NOT YOU HEARD GOD FOR SURE.**

Part II

SUPERNATURAL HEALINGS

(Mine and Others)

Front Page News

There are many things of which the Lord has healed me, most being inward attitudes and emotions. What I want to tell you about now, however, is a couple of times that the Lord supernaturally healed me physically.

After church one Sunday afternoon, I was sitting on my couch reading a book. While still sitting I fell asleep with my legs in a crossed position. I suddenly awoke because I needed to go to the bathroom. I quickly jumped up and took about three or four steps, and then my right ankle just bent. It felt as if the leg bowed, and sounded as if a two-by-four had been broken in half. I fell to the floor in agonizing pain. I was rushed to the emergency room at the hospital where they took many x-rays. The bone specialist on duty that day came in and told me that I had fractures and breaks, and that the bones would have to be set and then put in a large cast. He said I must wear it for eight weeks, at which time, if all was well, they would take off that cast and put on a walking cast for another six to eight weeks. After the cast was on and dry, the doctor instructed me to, "Go home, elevate your leg, and keep ice packs on it for the next couple of days. Do not put pressure on that foot or leg!"

Believe it or not, I did not want to go home. I wanted to go back to church. So that's what I did but I arrived late. It was with great difficulty that I was trying to manage crutches and a leg that was becoming fully alive to pain. (The pain medication was wearing off.) Before I could reach the seating area I heard our pastor announce that we were changing the course of the

God'sidences (God's Intervention Today)

service and, instead of our usual order, we would have a healing service right then!

He came down from behind the podium and pushed a chair up behind me so that I was forced to sit. Then he brought another chair in front and helped me lift my leg onto it. Next he instructed the congregation to gather around me. They did, even the little children.

They all began to lay hands on me and pray. It was the children, though, who laid their hands upon the cast. It was at that moment, I knew God healed the leg. I did not feel different, but I knew. (GOD'SIDENCE!)

When I got home that evening, indeed I did get ice packs and lie down with the leg elevated. Then the wrestling began. "I know you healed it Lord, so what do I do?" I finally fell asleep about midnight. When morning came I once again was wrestling with my thoughts. By evening (26 hours after receiving prayer) I knew what I was going to do.

Early the next morning, upon rising, I retrieved the hammer, wire cutters, screwdrivers, and several other tools from their storage drawer and started taking off the cast. I feel rather foolish now because I spent so much time hacking away at that cast, when all I would have had to do was soak it off. Live and learn. Of course, the whole time I was working at getting it off, I also had to face great opposition and ridicule from my husband. He really did think I was nuts. "I'm telling you, God has healed it!"

After removing the cast, I took a shower and got dressed up, high heels and all. I drove to the specialist's office, parked, and went in. The doctor saw me coming and hurried toward me, saying, "What have you done?" I was so excited that right there in the waiting area, which was just inside the front door, I yelled, "Don't you know God heals today just like He did

Front Page News

yesterday!" He quickly got me to the x-ray machine and took all new pictures. When viewing them, he compared the pictures from two days prior with the new ones. Shaking his head, he said, "Look! There is no indication, not one, that a break or fracture occurred, ever! It is a miracle!" (GOD'SIDENCE!) IT WAS COMPLETELY HEALED! The only evidence that any injury had occurred was the discoloration of the skin from the bleeding that had been inside.

As a result, the doctor contacted the newspaper and told them of the miracle. The story was published on the front page. (GOD'SIDENCE!)

It Disappeared

This is the second major physical healing that the Lord bestowed upon me. I had been in church about three years when I started having pain in the back of my head. I prayed personally at first, but then sought out the Elders to anoint me with oil and pray a prayer of faith. Although they did, the pain persisted. Finally I went to the doctor. He sent me to a specialist who examined me and performed several tests. His answer was, "Glorian, you need to have a further testing done. You will have to go to Seattle to the University of Washington Medical Center where they have the equipment. You have a tumor at the base of your skull. It is not a matter of whether or not you have one, you do. It is a matter of how big is it and what kind is it?" I replied to him that it was not possible at that time to have any expensive tests done, for I had no insurance and no finances. I left crying and scared. Jesus was the only One Who could help me.

Two weeks later I returned to the specialist. The situation remained the same. I continued to return every two to three weeks for several months. Each time the doctor pleaded with me to have the tests done, and each time I left not knowing what to do.

At that time our pastor was holding evangelistic crusades throughout our county. Of course, I attended them all because I was the altar worker. One night we were holding one of these crusades in Alger, a small community nearby. We had secured the Alger Community Building. I was at the altar working when suddenly I fell backward and hit my head on the floor

It Disappeared

. . . so hard that the whole meeting was disrupted. I remember hearing the sound of my head hitting the floor but there was no feeling. I did not have any knot nor pain from the impact, and "No," I was not in the process of receiving prayer. (GOD'SIDENCE!)

The next week I went to the doctor as usual. Upon examining me, he loudly proclaimed that the TUMOR WAS GONE! (GOD'SIDENCE!) I was so excited when I left his office that I ran across the street to the clinic where I had to have mammograms every six months because I had white spots on both breasts, which usually indicate the beginning of cancer. (On my biological father's side of the family, all the women have breast cancer.) I insisted they do another mammogram, although it had only been a few weeks since the last one. HEALED! SPOTS GONE! (GOD'SIDENCE!)

The 700 Club

Now here's the kicker (the devil roams about seeking whom he may devour). Several years later I began to experience pain in my head once again. My first thoughts were that the tumor had returned. I wrestled with those thoughts for several weeks. One night I left the office a little later than normal (by that time I was an associate minister in our church), went home, changed my clothes, and then cut myself a slice of watermelon. Taking my food with me, I proceeded to the small room where we kept the television set. I turned it on to the *700 club*, a Christian program. Then while sitting on the sofa, I began eating my melon as I watched the program. Pat Robertson was praying for people. Shortly thereafter he picked up a letter and read it aloud. The prayer request so touched my heart that I felt compelled to get off the sofa and kneel on the floor. I set my plate of melon on the floor beside me and in tears I began to intercede for the author of the letter. When Pat finished praying, he looked into the camera and said, "There is a woman out in the TV audience who just got on her knees to pray with us, and she set her plate of food on the floor beside her. God says to tell you, 'YOU DO NOT HAVE A BRAIN TUMOR!'" Can you imagine my shock and my elation? Do you really think that could be anything other than God? No way! **IT WAS ABSOLUTELY A GOD'SIDENCE!**

At this point I want to tell you that there are other physical healings that I still need. I confess I do not understand why the Lord touches and heals some things and not others. Nor do I understand His timing in this area. All I know is that I trust Him and whether He heals me now, or down the road or not at all this side of heaven, yet I will serve Him and Him alone. He is good!

As you read these pages, please understand that most healing miracles that have occurred when I was praying for someone have happened without my knowledge of it at the moment. (I said most, not all!) It was strictly God's doing after I was gone. We are instructed in the Word to lay hands on the sick and pray a prayer of faith for healing, which is what we must do, regardless of outcome. I do not consider myself "a healer." I do consider myself a Christian simply doing the best I can to be obedient at any given moment. I do believe fully that **when our hearts are "moved with compassion" that it is the work of the Lord Jesus Christ urging us to be available at that moment.**

I know some of you will say, "Yeah, but what about people who are not Christians that suddenly have compassion rise within?" I still believe it is Jesus, because man was created in the image of God. Saved or unsaved, mankind still has the breath of God in him.

A Lady in Waiting

I must have been in church for about three years when I attended a two-day conference in Stanwood, Washington. When the break came between sessions, I left the front row and started walking down the center aisle toward the back entrance. As I was walking, I happened to notice a lady sitting on an aisle seat with one of her legs propped up onto a chair that was in front of her. She was wearing pants but the hem on the propped up leg was mid-calf in length. Her leg was horribly swollen and black and blue in color. It looked incredibly painful! Before I even had time to think about it, tears were running down my face and my heart felt broken for her condition. (GOD'SIDENCE!) I remember quickly kneeling and gingerly touching her stretched skin and asking the Lord to heal her. She thanked me as I got up, then we hugged and off I went. I did not see her again for the remainder of the conference.

It was almost a year later when I received a telephone call at the church, where, at the time, I was the church secretary. The lady on the other end started asking me questions. "Did you go to a conference at Warm Beach in Stanwood about a year ago? Were you part of the team with the speaker? Were you the lady who bent down and prayed for a lady with a swollen black and blue leg?" On and on she went until she was assured that I was the right lady and that I remembered the incident. "I have spent much time trying to locate you," she said. "I've been trying to find you so I could share the miracle that happened as a result of the prayer you prayed for me. God healed me! [GOD'SIDENCE!] I was supposed to have surgery on that leg. I was already scheduled for the surgery that would have been just a short while after the conference." We cried together over the telephone, **both of us recognizing that it was the heart of Jesus, full of compassion that suddenly flowed from with one of His own out to another of His beloved ones and touched her.** I can take no credit; for almost a year I didn't even know that she had been healed or that she had been scheduled for surgery.

A Hospital Run

Another time there was a man in the hospital who occasionally attended our fellowship. He happened to be friends with one of my neighbors. One evening, my neighbors requested that I go with them to visit their friend and pray for him. I agreed.

While at the hospital visiting with the man I noticed his roommate, which, of course was another gentleman. The roommate looked in really terrible condition. He was in a body cast, leg casts, in traction, plus his head was immobilized and wrapped in bandages. I asked him what had happened. The story was that he had been riding on top of a full semi-truck load of bundled hay. For whatever reason, he had stood up while the truck was traveling at full speed down the freeway. Of course, he could not keep his balance and fell off! His body was broken everywhere, and he was scheduled for surgery on his head within hours. When he had fallen, he hit his head on the pavement so hard that it was full of blood and fluid that was going to cause his death if something wasn't done soon. Even then, there was the great possibility that he would die anyway.

At the time of the visit, I was able to talk to the man for only a few moments but found out that he was not a Christian. He told me that he was an atheist. I laughed and told him he wasn't. I told him it was only that he had not yet met Jesus. I informed him I would like to pray for him. He smiled as he declined the invitation. I did not believe him. The Lord filled

A Hospital Run

me with compassion for that man, and so as I was leaving the room a short while later, I stopped at the foot of his bed, took hold of his big toe, and simply asked, "Lord, please heal him so that he would know You are real." The man said nothing; he only stared at me.

As with the previous story, I again did not know, until well after the fact, that God, indeed, miraculously, healed his head and no surgery was needed. (GOD'SIDENCE!) The report was that the doctors completely were shocked that his head was healed. The mending of his bones took the normal amount of time.

I never heard from the man himself, but the report came from my neighbor's friend, who had been the roommate in the hospital. He reported that they spent much time talking about the Lord after the miracle occurred.

The Young and the Old Can Come to Jesus

Another time, back in about 1991 or so, while ministering in a northern city of Poland, God did a miracle! The church was a new fellowship in its beginning stages. They had put together a two-day evangelistic crusade for the city. Perhaps 60 to 80 people came to those meetings. That was a lot in those days. On the second night, the invitation was issued to all those who would like to accept Jesus as their personal Savior. The whole altar filled. I remember one very precious old man who had been a Catholic his whole life. He came forward and accepted Jesus as his personal Savior. I remember him in particular because it is so very unusual for someone as old as he was to change his way of believing. (I am not saying that Catholics do not love Jesus. It is simply that they get a greater revelation of Who Jesus is after accepting Him as their personal Savior.) After those who had come forward for salvation had received prayer, we issued a second altar call for those who would like healing in their bodies. Again the altar filled, though not so many, and again the old man came forward. I remember him in particular. With each of those for whom I was praying there was not enough time to have every need interpreted and then to have the prayer interpreted in return. So I simply went down the line and stood in front of each person and prayed the way that I felt led by the Holy Spirit to pray. When I came to the old man, I did not know what was wrong with him but I felt

The Young and the Old Can Come to Jesus

great compassion rise within my heart for him. (It was unusual for an old man to come to an altar, and here he was a second time, right after just getting saved!) I remember simply laying my hand upon the front portion of his shoulder and praying a simple prayer, asking God to intervene and heal whatever was wrong.

The next time I was in Poland, the young pastor of that fellowship, who had held the crusade, took me aside and said, "Glo, you remember old man you pray for? One who got Jesus? One who came to healing, too?" I replied that I did remember. "God do a miracle! The old man my Great Papa (grandfather). He have cancer in whole body! When we go to take hospital, he not come. Great Papa say, 'No! First I give Jesus one week!'" What transpired during that week was that on his shoulder (the spot where I happened—not by revelation—to lay my hand during prayer), a boil began to form. It grew so big (as a small melon) that it broke and puss ran from it in huge quantities. According to the young pastor, the doctors had reported later that the cancer had localized in that shoulder and poured forth as puss. He was healed! Jesus did it! (GOD'SIDENCE!)

The old man died about a year or two later. He died a normal, peaceful death with no diseases. To God, is all the glory!

Beyond Medical Knowledge

I love this story about the Lord's intervention. Years ago as I was walking down the main street of Mount Vernon, Washington, there was a pregnant lady (about eight months along) walking toward me. As she passed by, the thought came to me that she was having twins and something was wrong with one of them. Strange thought, huh? I walked on a bit further but was uneasy inside. I did not feel right about going on by and not addressing the issue with this lady. I know you know the process, "But God, what if I'm wrong?" After reasoning for a moment, I decided to throw caution to the wind and turned to find her. I began yelling for her to stop. She turned and realized I was calling to her, so she stopped and waited for me to catch up with her. When reaching her, I spoke something to the effect of, "Excuse me, please, I know this is going to seem very unusual to you. I am a Christian and I believe God just spoke to my heart that you are having twins and there is a problem. I need to pray for the babies and for you." (GOD'SIDENCE!)

She started turning red with embarrassment but said to me, "No, I am only having one." "Please, I really need to do this!" I begged. She then informed me that she had already had several ultra sounds showing only one child, plus there was only one heartbeat!

Although she was very conscious of the people who were watching us, she finally allowed me to pray. I bent down and began addressing the children in her womb. Then I prayed for the mother, too. Having finished I left.

Beyond Medical Knowledge

Years later, after having moved away from that county, I returned to visit with friends who hold meetings in their home. One of the ladies attending that evening was a casual acquaintance whom I had not seen in several years. When she saw me, she got excited and proclaimed, "Glo, I have to tell you about a friend of mine who lives in Anacortes. A few months ago we were visiting, and we got on the subject of how the Lord had intervened supernaturally into our lives and into the lives of our children." She then proceeded to relay to me the story told to her by her friend.

"My friend told me about an incident when she was walking down the street in Mount Vernon, Washington. There she was stopped by a red-headed woman stating she was a Christian, and then told her she was going to have twins and that she needed to pray." That lady recognized God's hand upon her life and the lives of her children AFTER SHE BIRTHED TWINS! (GOD'SIDENCE!) You know the rest of the story! The lady telling me the story said she told her friend, "I know this lady, her name is Glo, and the next time I see her I will let her know." (GOD'SIDENCE!)

God is very gracious, kind, and loving. He did not have to let me know that the lady actually had birthed twins, but in doing so I was greatly encouraged, in a season when I needed to be encouraged. I also was very grateful . . . grateful for His intervention in their lives and grateful that He tugs at our hearts to be obedient. I think about it now and am overcome with joy because there is a life that was saved because of God's intervention!

A Strange Event
(In the old training ground)

If you will recall, as the years progressed I was Department Head over several areas in our church. At one point I became the church secretary. It was a time which tested the very fiber of my being. The Church to which God sent me was never an easy place for me to be. I loved church! I loved my pastor, and I loved the people! But I also had a difficult time being accepted by some of the people (though not by my pastor— he was always for me). I faced situations that in no way were the norm. Let me give you an example. When I had been in church for about one year, one of the men walked up to me and said these exact words: "I know in Christ I'm supposed to love you, but I can't stand your guts!" Then he just walked away. I was devastated. What did I do? It made no sense whatsoever. I was torn and had to wrestle with it.

A few months later he came back to me and said, "I'm sorry, I don't know why I did that." (GOD'SIDENCE!) Of course, I had not yet gained much wisdom and was too frequently telling about the miracles that God was doing (which did not win me friends)!

There were also two ladies in particular who took an immediate disliking to me. One never did get over her dislike and actively persecuted me until her death. On several occasions the other one stood before the congregation and admitted she was jealous of me. At those times my heart would break for her, even though I did not want to be in her presence. She spoke

A Strange Event

to me in cutting ways that caused me great pain and stress. (Please bear in mind that I was from an abusive background and could be wounded more easily than perhaps others may have been in some of the same situations.)

Well, as God would have it, I was required to serve as the church secretary for two years. My boss was the church administrator, who also happened to be the very same lady who disliked me so much and admitted to jealousy. (GOD'SIDENCE!) Almost every day I would go to work and leave in tears by the end of the day. I begged God to release me from that job. After all, it was not even a paying job, I reasoned, but I could not deny that God had put me there.

As the weeks and months went by, I felt so battered and beat up that I prayed and prayed asking for an answer to why I had to work under this lady. One day the Lord answered me: "I am teaching you to walk in love, no matter what comes your way!" That I could accept and even had some revelation concerning the lengths to which God will go to teach us and to transform our hearts. Understanding the spiritual significance of what was happening helped, even if it did not stop the pain. I COULD RECOGNIZE, THOUGH, THAT MY REACTIONS WERE CHANGING WEEKLY! (GOD'SIDENCE!)

The administrator's office was at the top of the stairs on the second floor of the building, while the secretary's office was at the foot of the stairs on the main floor. Inside my office, my desk was facing the stairs, as well as the doors into the building. Through a large glass window I had a complete view of everyone coming and going. One day I looked up and there was the administrator literally stomping down the stairs with anger on her face. I knew she was coming toward me. "Oh, God, what now?" Almost before I could finish my question to the Lord, she hit the door and caused it to bang against the wall. I stood up but before I could say anything she was screaming.

Suddenly the Lord supernaturally intervened and it became as though a glass bubble or dome had been placed over me, and I no longer could hear her. (GOD'SIDENCE!) I do not know what she said because her words became visible but scrambled. The words were proceeding from out of her mouth, hitting the barrier and traveling around it in two directions.

I was in shock! Then all of a sudden there was an overwhelming love in my heart for this woman. (GOD'SIDENCE!) I reached out with my arms and encircled her and began to sob, "I love you so much!" She struggled at first and then her body went limp. She began to sob also. From that day on we have been friends. That does not mean that all has been perfect, but from that point we could work out the differences.

A few years later God tested us even further by moving her into my home for a season. Yes, we got along. She is a wonderful woman and called by God! As a matter of fact, we even went on a few missions together.

I dare say that the greatest lessons I have learned have come about through the most difficult relationships I've experienced.

Without opposition in our lives, we never would know the fruit of the Holy Spirit, in which we are aspiring to mature. In other words, we want to be as Jesus and walk in love, joy, peace, patience, kindness, goodness, faithfulness, gentleness, and self-control. (Gal. 5:22) **This should not be something we are "trying" to do, but a reality that has been worked into the very fiber of our beings.**

Part III

"WORDS," VISIONS, and EVENTS

The Toaster Plug Cover

I really used to enjoy my morning toast with a cup of fresh coffee. It was quick, easy, and enough as I prepared to tackle the challenges of a new day. My morning routine was well established. Upon arising, I would walk into the kitchen, set the coffee to brewing. and then reach for my faithful and trusted old toaster. Now this was no ordinary toaster by modern standards. It was a 1950's model made of stainless steel with sleek, well-rounded corners and curves. There was substance to this toaster. It was heavy and built to last a lifetime. Of course, I don't think the designers or engineers reckoned on the advent of plastics for electrical appliances or rubber cords or the changes in design for wall outlets. Mine had a cord wrapped in a cloth material and at its end was a large round plug with two prongs of the exact same size. Today electrical cords are made of rubber and the plugs are small and square with two prongs of different sizes.

One morning, in a rather rushed state, I set about my morning routine. As I reached for the toaster plug and connected it to the wall outlet, an immediate sharp crackling sizzling sound exploded into the atmosphere, accompanied by flames shooting out from the wall. I quickly pulled on the cord, removing the plug from the outlet. The wall was left with black streaks and I was left with fear! Quickly I called the fire department and then began to beseech the Lord, though I knew not for what to pray. There were all kinds of thoughts running through my mind. "Is the house on fire? How fast can they get here? Help, Lord!"

God'sidences (God's Intervention Today)

Soon the firemen arrived, quickly looked the situation over, and with amusement pronounced their conclusion. "Lady, your plug has no cover!" They went on to explain that the wires had worked their way loose and directly had come into contact with the power source when I started to plug it into the outlet.

Now, I had been using that toaster for several years without the plug being covered. As a matter of fact, I don't believe the cover was on it when it was given to me as a replacement for mine that had gone "kaput." The toaster had been someone's "old stand by," should their updated model ever malfunction . . . but when I was in need, they graciously passed it on.

Well, as the story goes, several days passed with me trying to carry out my morning routine but, of course, when it came time to plug in the toaster I would remember that I could not. Finally I stopped trying. Though I made a mental note that I needed to go to some secondhand stores and see if I could locate an old plug cover, I was doubtful if I would have success finding one. Several weeks passed and I simply never got around to setting time aside to pursue the task.

Summer was in full swing, and the weather was extremely hot when one afternoon a young man came to see me at my office for some counseling. (I was an associate minister in my church.) My office was on the second floor, had neither windows nor air conditioning, and was very stuffy. I suggested that we go into the large meeting room next door which had lots of windows and a fire escape door. We proceeded to open all the windows on both sides of the room, plus the fire escape door, so as to get a cross draft if possible.

We then pulled up two chairs facing each other, with my back toward the windows, and about three feet behind me and to my right from the fire escape door.

The Toaster Plug Cover

After about ten minutes of talking, I noticed a slight breeze began to blow periodically, and over the next few minutes it became stronger. Suddenly, out of the corner of my eye, I noticed something blowing into the room on the wind. I thought it was a dried leaf, brown and faded. It entered in through the door at about eye height where **it began its downward descent until it landed right on top of my right foot!** (GOD'SIDENCE!)

I screamed in excitement (and scared the young man) as I beheld a round plug cover with two prong openings of the same size! My excitement was not containable as I jumped to my feet and began to yell, "You don't understand! God has sent me a toaster plug cover!" God had just done a miraculous thing!

Where did He get it? How long was it in the wind? How many days, weeks, or even years had it been traveling to get to me? Was it really the wind that carried it in or was it an angel? GOD CARED!

I raced home to see if it fit my toaster and, of course, it did. To this day I wonder how the Lord did that? I can tell you this much with all confidence. God divinely intervenes into the lives of His own.

The Z28 Camaro

One Sunday as we drove into the parking lot at our church, I had this thought come to me (seemingly from out of nowhere): "See that car?" "Yes, Lord," I answered. "I am going to cause the man who owns it to give it to you." I turned to my husband and told him what the Lord had just shared with me, and he laughed at me and told me I was crazy. I never had seen the car before, so I was not sure who owned it. Of course, I soon was to find that it belonged to a young man who recently had started attending our church. I never had seen him drive that car before because he usually drove a pick-up truck. I found out that he rarely drove the car and kept it in the garage with a car blanket covering it. It was his pride and joy.

That car was beautiful. It was a rich, chocolate brown color with little bits of gold flecking in the paint. It had a removable smoked glass T-top and leather interior with sheepskin covers. The engine was big! It was a man's car . . . not the sort of car I would have chosen for myself.

As the months progressed, I started to forget about it. It had been almost a year since the day the Lord had spoken to me concerning that car.

During that year I still was working as an associate minister at the church. One evening we were going to have a special guest speaker. Our pastor was out of town that day but would return late in the afternoon. The telephone rang and it was a man calling to cancel the speaker's engagement. Seems that on their way to our church, she had taken ill and needed to be hospitalized.

The Z28 Camaro

A couple of hours passed by, and I heard the Holy Spirit say, "This is a supernatural miracle-making day, record it." (GOD'SIDENCE!) A little while later I heard Him say, "Blow the trumpet!" I went downstairs to the sanctuary and got a trumpet and blew it in four directions. While still in there, the Lord said, "Anoint every chair in the congregation." (GOD'SIDENCE!) I was starting to get excited . . . what was the Lord doing? I was about half finished with the chairs when a brother from our congregation bounded in the door and stated: "The Lord has sent me to anoint every seat in the orchestra." (GOD'SIDENCE!) I explained what the Lord was having me do and we both got excited. It was only a few moments later when the outside **locked side doors to the sanctuary opened!** (GOD'SIDENCE!) There was no human being there. What happened was not possible except for God! Instantly the room began to fill with a sweet fragrance. (GOD'SIDENCE!) Both my brother and I stood looking at one another in awe and wonder. He said to me, "You didn't do that, did you?" No, I had not. I was on the other side of the room, no where near the doors. The doors slowly closed and once again they were locked.

I ran out of the sanctuary, into the lobby, and took a few deep breaths. Then I went back inside and, sure enough, the room was filled with the sweet fragrance of flowers such as lilies, honeysuckle, jasmine and gardenias, and . . . .

I was so sure that something amazing was about to happen that I went back to my office and called the man who runs the video camera on special occasions. "Set it up, Doug, this is going to be a supernatural miracle-making night!"

At about five o'clock, our pastor returned and I relayed the message about our guest speaker not coming. "What are we going to do?" he asked. "Don't worry about it because God told

God'sidences (God's Intervention Today)

me that this is a miracle-making day!" I also told him that I had called Doug to set up the cameras.

Service time rolled around and we had a large crowd that night. The orchestra started playing for the song service portion of our meeting. In the midst of it, the Lord instructed me: "Go and kneel between the door and the congregation." (GOD'SIDENCE!) So I got up and went behind the congregation and knelt down. **Suddenly a mighty rushing Wind cut right through me** from my right side to the left. It circled the whole room and then rushed through me again. Over and over it circled! Each time it would rush through me, tears would leap out of my eyes, and I would feel as if I couldn't catch my breath. It was miraculous! (GOD'SIDENCE!)

After awhile of the Wind rushing around the room, people began to speak and confess their sins! (GOD'SIDENCE!) Some lives were forevermore changed that night.

Finally, the Wind stopped circling the room and the song service stopped. The pastor got up and said, "Well, ladies and gentleman, I think we have had our service for this evening." You could hear the buzz as people began to whisper, not understanding why. He directed everyone's attention to the time. **More than four hours had passed!** (GOD'SIDENCE!) It felt as if only 20 or 30 minutes had gone by, which was the normal span of time we would have been singing.

I do not know how others felt inside but as I got up from my knees, I felt completely exhausted and so in love with Jesus!

As I started to leave the sanctuary, the Lord spoke to me saying, "I am giving you three gifts!"

As soon as I had left the sanctuary and was in the lobby, a sister in the Lord walked toward me and said, "Here, Glo, I thought you might like a video of your Ordination Service." **There was one gift!** Before I could get across the lobby, a brother came and handed me some money, saying, "The Lord just spoke to me to give you this." **There was the second gift!** By the time I opened the door to go outside, the Lord spoke again and said, "And the car!" That did it, I knew that I had heard right a year earlier!

I drove home and walked into the house and reported to my husband that I really knew the car was going to be given to me because of everything that had happened that evening. Of course, my husband did not believe it really would happen. By all appearances, he was correct, because he came home a couple of days later and began to taunt me, saying, "I saw your car on the lot of a new dealership today. It is for sale." "I don't care, I know I heard God!"

One month later on a Saturday morning, my husband and I were sitting in the kitchen when the young man who owned the car knocked on our back door. We motioned him to come on in. When he came through the door, he marched straight over to the counter and laid down the keys, title, and registration. "Here, I am giving you my car. I am sick and tired of being disobedient to God!" he said.

The look on my husband's face was one of absolute shock!

The young man went on to say, "Now, this is how I see it. You can take *your* car and sell it and *this* car and sell it and then buy yourself a brand new car to travel in while you minister." Out of my mouth flew the words, "Are you crazy? I'm not selling the car God gave me!" Instantly it was as if I were being slapped in the face with a cold rag. (GOD'SIDENCE!) "Oh, God, forgive me. I don't even know why You have given me this car." It never occurred to me why the Lord may have given it to me.

The next morning as I was driving to church in the Z28, I began to cry at the amazing way the Lord does things. "Lord, why did You give me this car?" "Because every time you look

God'sidences (God's Intervention Today)

upon it and every time you step upon the accelerator, I want you to remember My power to bring about those things which I have spoken to you and those things which I have shown you!" He said. (GOD'SIDENCE!)

Please realize this, **the Lord gave me the car as a reprimand and a reminder.**

There are many things the Lord has shared with me, and shown me, which, in the natural, seem impossible but I remember the Z28, and I am reminded of His great power to bring those things to pass. God is so good!

I always am amazed at the way the Lord maneuvers the circumstances around us to fulfill His plans and purposes.

The Giving Man

The young man who gave me his Z28 told me that when the Lord had instructed him to give it to me, he prayed and asked confirmation. When he believed he had received it, he went to his new wife to share with her what the Lord had instructed. She told him that she would rather put the car up for sale and use the money from it to put a down payment on a home. Because they were not in agreement, they chose to put the car on the lot for sale. If you recall from earlier in this story, the car just sat there with no buyers. He still felt as if he had heard the Lord and once again approached his wife. They prayed and decided to put a fleece before the Lord. Together they made a list with many items on it. Then they each made a separate list with many items on each one. You know the kind. "Lord, if that's really you . . . then make such and such happen," etc.

The Lord met every condition on all three lists, at which point they no longer could deny that it was God instructing them. I always will be grateful for their obedience, because God used it to propel me into the European continent; Poland was only the beginning.

Checks, Checks, and More Checks

One morning as I awoke and opened my eyes, I saw checks floating in the air in my room. The closest check to me was in the amount of $10,000. Quickly I saw others with differing amounts on them.

I blinked my eyes a couple of times and the room was normal... no checks. I knew deep within me that I just had seen something from God.

I went to work (at the church) and proclaimed that we needed to check the mail as soon as possible. Of course, upon explanation everyone thought I was crazy. But, I knew God had shown me something and believed He was about to send me $10,000. (GOD'SIDENCE!)

For two years every day I watched the mail for the money.

During that time, I went on a 10-day trip with my sister and her husband as they drove long-haul across the USA. They were both semi-truck drivers and worked as a team for several years after their children had become adults. Two supernatural events transpired during that trip.

The first was after several days of being on the road. We pulled off at a truck stop to fill up the fuel tank and to eat. As we were walking across the parking lot toward the restaurant, a lady came running up to me and said, "Don't move, I'll be right back!" She ran to her vehicle and right back, declaring, "Hold out your hand! **God said to tell you this is the down payment on the $10,000 that is on its way!**" As she said it, she laid a single dime in my hand. (GOD'SIDENCE!)

Checks, Checks, and More Checks

Yes, it did come! (GOD'SIDENCE!)

It was used to pay for a couple of ministers to travel overseas, in addition a trip for me. God also instructed me to pay for a man's entire mouth to be fixed with teeth. (Today he ministers in Europe and the USA.) (GOD'SIDENCE!)

A lady needed to have her teeth fixed, as well, because hers were so bad that they were poisoning her system causing cancer. She'd already had one surgery. The Lord instructed me that as I gave her the money, I was to tell her, "God said this is the last time." I learned it was the third time she had been given the money to have her teeth fixed but she always used the money given to her to help others with great needs. She now pastors a church. (GOD'SIDENCE!)

It also supplied new contacts for a young lady who had eyeglasses so thick that she appeared deformed . . . it changed her life! (GOD'SIDENCE!)

The second thing that happened on that road trip was that the Lord gave me a word for my sister and her husband. "Beware of Navajo!" "What does that mean?" they asked. "I don't know" was all I could tell them.

Some time went by and the company for which they worked was going to be purchased by a company named "Navajo." Remembering the word from the Lord to "beware," they both retired from that company and took their benefits. (GOD'SIDENCE!) The people who continued working as the company changed owners lost all their benefits.

God intervened in the lives of my sister and brother-in-law and saved them from a disaster in the making.

Dreams
(Night Visions)

I have many dreams that are prophetic in nature. I also have those that guide me when faced with decisions.

I would like to share a series of dreams that were prophetic concerning my life.

It was 1988 and I would awaken with a Scripture address being repeated in my dream. I did not know what those Scriptures said, but I would record the address on a piece of paper I kept on my nightstand. This went on for six months. One day the thought occurred to me that, "Perhaps God is trying to write me a letter." (GOD'SIDENCE!) I took the paper downstairs to my typewriter, and one by one I looked them up and typed them as I found them. They were II Tim. 4:1-5 . . . Ez. 2:4 . . . Mic. 6:1 . . . Mic. 1:6 . . . Is. 54:2-3

When typed out and personalized, it reads:

> "Glo, I solemnly charge you in the presence of God and of Christ Jesus, Who is to judge the living and the dead, and by His appearing and His Kingdom: Preach the Word, be ready in season and out of season; reprove, rebuke, exhort, with great patience and instruction. For the time will come when they will not endure sound doctrine; but wanting to have their ears tickled, they will accumulate for themselves teachers in accordance to their own desires; and will turn aside to myths. But you, Glo, be

sober in all things, endure hardships, do the work of an evangelist, fulfill your ministry . . . for "I am sending you to them who are stubborn and obstinate children; and you shall say to them, 'Thus says the Lord God!' As for them, whether or not they listen–for they are a rebellious house–they will know that a prophet has been among them." Hear now what the Lord is saying: "Arise, plead your case before the mountains and let the hills hear your voice . . . for I will make Samaria a heap of ruins in the open country, planting places for a vineyard. I will pour her stones down into the valley and will lay bare her foundations. Enlarge the place of your tent; stretch out the curtains of your dwellings, spare not; lengthen your cords and strengthen your pegs. For you will spread abroad to the right and to the left, and your descendants will possess nations, and they will resettle desolate cities." (GOD'SIDENCE!)

It, indeed, was a prophetic letter to me from my "Father Who art in Heaven." Has it come to pass? Yes. (GOD'SIDENCE!) Today the curtains of my dwelling are in 40 nations of the world. I certainly spread to the left and the right. And those I have trained and mentored are in ministry all over the world.

Please understand, I did not set out to make things happen . . . to fulfill the prophecy. **God did it all!** I simply take each new step He gives me. We only can live in today.

Pay attention to your dreams. The Lord often speaks to us through them.

Visions
(Internal Pictures)

For the next several pages, I am going to tell you of a few of the pictures the Lord has placed within my head and the subsequent results.

Once at a conference, during my earlier years as a Christian, we were instructed to break into small groups and pray for one another. There were about six or seven in the group with which I was joined. I knew none of them. As we formed a circle and held hands, I closed my eyes. As soon as I did, I saw the letter "C" and then a picture of a river boat with a large paddle wheel. It was navigating up a river. I certainly did not expect a vision but wanted to test it as to whether or not it was from the Lord. So daring to speak, I opened my mouth and said, "The Lord shows me there is someone, I believe it is a man, whose name starts with a "C" and he has been fighting against the current." One of the ladies let out a scream, "That's my husband, Charlie! He is! He is fighting against everything the Lord has placed before him!" (GOD'SIDENCE!) That opened our hearts to intercede for Charlie.

Another time the Lord instructed us to do an unusual task, which we, as a team, could not have completed if He had not given visions.

Part of a mission to the USA (1989-1990) included going to Hawaii. First, we needed to accomplish the original assignment, which was to blow a trumpet, repent, pray, prophesy and take communion at the border of every state in the USA. (The whole story will be written in another book.)

Visions

Just prior to our departure from the mainland to Hawaii, we went to Seattle to visit with a friend of ours, Sherry Lorenzen, from the Youth With A Mission organization (YWAM for short—pronounced Y-WAM). We sat telling her of all the God'sidences that had transpired thus far during our mission. We also told her of our need concerning the upcoming leg of the mission, Hawaii.

She got excited and said she knew a pilot who had been posted in Hawaii, and maybe he could help us find a guide and helper. She picked up the telephone, called him, and arranged for us all to go to his home and meet with him later that afternoon. (GOD'SIDENCE!) "His name is Mike Lewis." she informed us.

We laid out all the information before Mike, telling him we were leaving on a Friday morning and returning the following Monday morning. (We had told Mike that the Lord had instructed us to: "Get in, take care of business, and get out!" which had not made a lot of sense to us.) He shook his head and stated that he did not see how anything could be accomplished in such a short time. As we prayed, the Lord spoke to Mike's heart and informed him that He was sending us to do a "surgical strike". (GOD'SIDENCE!) Mike told us what the Lord had said, then went on to explain that this is a term used by the military which means soldiers are sent in quietly to defuse the enemies weapons. Then we understood.

Mike gave us the name and telephone number of a friend, Robin Disque, who was also with YWAM and still stationed in Hawaii. He informed us that he would call and tell him everything.

Just prior to our flight to Hawaii, the Lord gave us an added assignment. He said, "I want you to take communion in twelve strategic locations around the Island."

God'sidences (God's Intervention Today)

Arriving in Hawaii, we called Robin from the airport. He came and picked us up and drove us to our hotel. He informed us that was all he could do to help us because he had a time restraint. We thanked him for the ride and were prepared to rent a vehicle and take care of business.

We bought a map of the Island and then spent several hours mulling over it and praying. We needed to hear from the Lord as to where these twelve places were located, plus we needed to know where the "border" location would be. Everyone had different ideas and suggestions as to where these places were located; each with good reason in the natural, but what we needed was information from God!

When given a task, following the Holy Spirit is our first order of business, because His ways are always higher than ours are.

Finally, after much deliberation, we decided to go to bed and continue to seek His leading in the morning.

Just before retiring for the evening Robin, called and told us that the Lord had dealt with him (severely) and told him he was to serve us and treat us as royalty—that he was to be at our beck and call! (GOD'SIDENCE!)

Morning came and Robin was there early to pick us up and take us to his home, where he proceeded to prepare a huge breakfast for us. While he was cooking, the team had the map laid out on the table and was still trying to figure out where these strategic places might be. All of a sudden, the thought struck me "around the Island!" (GOD'SIDENCE!) Our thinking had been "on" the island but the Lord had said "around" the island. Quickly I called to Robin to come for a moment and then asked him if there were twelve different people groups or types of activities around the edge of the island. He responded by looking at the map and dividing it into sections. Sure enough, there were exactly twelve! (GOD'SIDENCE!)

Immediately I closed my eyes and began to pray, and just as immediately the Lord began to give me visions (pictures inside my head). I quickly began to draw what the Lord was showing me. He gave me exactly 13 pictures and then stopped. Because the pictures were drawn, the whole team was able to recognize the spot in each area where we were to be in order to carry out the assignment. All twelve "strategic places," plus the border location! (GOD'SIDENCE!) It was exciting and so very accurate. We did not know what some of the items drawn actually were, until confronted with them before our faces.

Please note, I understand what a struggle you may have with believing that what you see in "picture form" inside your head is really a vision from God. Dare to believe! **Dare to believe you hear from Him!**

The Lord has given me the privilege of leading, working with, and training in the areas of daring to believe . . . about 55 teams over the years. In size they have ranged from three to 56. (I have "heard it all" when it comes to people thinking they can't hear from God or that they don't have visions.)

The Lord has taught me that it is important to make a safe place for people to learn and to practice. We can do this by understanding first that there is no shame in failure, because God is looking at the heart! God loves our desire to be obedient and then loves our act of trying. It is worship!

Rocks and Rebar

Back to visions. Another time when we were going on a prophetic prayer assignment (to the north gate of the world), the Lord gave us visions and words, but at the time they meant nothing to us. This was way back in 1991, and our assignment was to be carried out in Archangel, USSR. That was still in the time of communism, and just getting into the nation (and that particular city) was a major miracle. (GOD'SIDENCE!) God had called three of us to go physically on this mission but there were many more included in the team who would remain behind as the prayer support. (This was another time when the Lord instructed us to "get in and get out!")

As we sat before the Lord praying, He gave one of the team members instructions concerning rocks and the building of an altar. To me he gave a picture of the strangest structure with what appeared to be curled and squiggly pieces of something sticking out from it. I drew what I was seeing on a piece of paper. We were all stumped as to what it could possibly be.

It was late in the day when we three, plus our interpreter, finally arrived at our hotel in Archangel. Throughout the entire time it took us to get from the USA to Archangel, which was two weeks, we had been on the lookout for rocks, any rocks, so we could carry them with us to build an altar. None were to be found! We ate dinner and then went to our rooms for the evening. We met early the next morning to pray about where we were to go to carry out our prayer assignment. As we prayed, I had the distinct feeling that if we went to the back of the hotel, we would understand what to do next. (GOD'SIDENCE!) So, trustingly, we trudged to the back of the building. Then lo and behold, there it was, a massive mound of egg-sized rock that had been dumped there. (GOD'SIDENCE!) Also very near was the strange structure I had seen and drawn. It was giant in size and was a piece of cement from a highway bridge with re-bar sticking out of it! It was exactly as the Lord had shown to me. (GOD'SIDENCE!)

Please do not think that these pictures the Lord shows are lengthy in their appearance. They are not; they are fast and often just a flash before your eyes. One must cultivate recognizing them. Most of the time people see them but think it is nothing or that it is something of their own making.

Remember that once you begin to recognize or think that something may be from God, you must act upon it ***before*** you will know for sure. That's called training. Even if you have received multiple confirmations, **you still will not know for sure until after you have acted upon it.**

Swords Everywhere!

In 1991 the Lord spoke the word "Ireland" to me. I understood that I needed to focus my attention in prayer on—and for—that nation. As time went by, the Lord placed it upon my heart that He wanted me to go there. It was then time to get specific instructions. The instructions came quickly. I was to take a team to Cob, in southern Ireland, and we were to raise the banner through the night of October 31st. If you think this made sense to me, let me tell you, it did not! But often the things the Lord spoke to me made no sense at the time. Once it was settled in my heart that I was going, then prayer for a team was in order. The Lord laid several people on my heart, and I asked them if they would pray and see what the Lord would say concerning them and the mission. By the time to depart, we were a team of six, five women and one man, all ministers.

Next each team member began to pray for further instructions, as did I. (Please take note that when God puts a team together, each member has a part to play. It is not the leader's responsibility to know everything, unless, of course, God gave those specific instructions.) In praying for more of the pieces of the puzzle the only other thing I received was a quick picture of a sword stuck halfway into a stone. It made no sense to me. What was I supposed to do with it, push it in or pull it out? Not understanding what it was all about, I simply set it aside, knowing that if it meant something special the Lord would show me in His own time.

Swords Everywhere!

Departure day arrived and we were aboard the airplane. Once we were off the ground, we began to discuss what the Lord had spoken to each member. This was the first time we actually could meet as a team. We were from three different States, Washington, Oregon, and Idaho. Each, in turn, told what information the Lord had given them. Then Ted, one of the team members, asked me, "What else did the Lord give you?" "Nothing! Well wait—I did get this one picture of a sword stuck in a stone," I replied. "Oh, that is just like Excalibur!" Ted said. Out of my mouth I commented, "Excalibur who?" Ted laughed and said, "Not who, what! Excalibur is King Arthur's sword!" My reply was instant, "God would not be telling me about fairy tales." Little did I know!

One morning while in Ireland, I dropped my partial upper plate and the clasp broke off. I loudly spoke out, "Oh, no! What am I going to do now?" The plate would not stay in my mouth. My roommate asked me what was wrong, and when I had told her, she got really excited and started digging through her suitcase. "Look!" she proclaimed, as she produced a tube of Fixodent. (GOD'SIDENCE!) She proceeded to tell me that as she and her husband had been walking down an aisle in the drug store that she simply reached over and threw it into the basket with her other items to be purchased. He asked her why she was getting it and she told him that she did not know why.

How's that for God meeting your every need?

The mission was awesome, with GOD'SIDENCES on every turn! But for this time I am trying to focus on visions and swords, so I'll not continue now.

That was the first time anything having to do with swords ever had transpired in my midst or concerned me in any way that I could remember.

More Swords

Months later, the Lord had me take a team to South Africa on a prophetic mission to the South Gate of the world. When finished there, we were going to Zimbabwe, Africa, to preach. A month or so prior to the departure date I received a call from the pastor in Zimbabwe, telling me that the church had been bombed and the members were afraid and scattered. He said he was sorry, but did not believe it would be wise to come at that time. Hanging up the telephone, I realized that the time we would have spent in Zimbabwe we now could spend in Cornwall, England (since we would be stopping in London for transfer anyway). I had been given a cottage in Cornwall (GOD'SIDENCE!) but had not seen it yet. This would be the perfect time. I told the team and we began to seek the Lord's direction to see if He wanted us to go to Cornwall instead. We all believed the Lord said, "Yes."

Our focus during that time was to concentrate on the mission to South Africa, so we met for prayer on a regular basis. What was strange, though, is that throughout our prayer times the Lord kept giving us information and instructions concerning Cornwall. (GOD'SIDENCE!) Yes, He also gave us the needed information about South Africa.

It was during those prayer times that, once again, the Lord brought back the vision of a sword stuck in a stone. I still did not understand it but took note that the Lord was trying to—or about to—show me something! I decided that since the Lord kept showing us things concerning Cornwall, that I would see what I could find in our old encyclopedias. Until given the cottage, I never even had heard of Cornwall. When I started reading about it, under the heading of England, there were several references made about King Arthur and Cornwall. I was a bit stumped. As I continued to read, I came across a name that jumped out at me. The name was Harold Godwin (King). Instantly I proclaimed, "Wait a minute, I'm a Godwin!" My Grandmother was Maggie Godwin. (GOD'SIDENCE!)

I started inquiring of the Lord if there were a connection dealing with the name. Was the Lord trying to tell me that somehow I had authority on that soil? Or perhaps I had a right to be on that soil? It was all so very mysterious.

After we got home from our trip to South Africa and Cornwall, every time I turned around (or so it seemed), things were popping up dealing with swords! I was preaching in the south part of Seattle and a lady brought me a lapel pin that was a sword. From Texas came an oil painting of a sword.

Knighted
(With an Imaginary Sword)

Then while preaching in Salem, Oregon, a man bolted through the door about midway through the message, disrupting the whole ssembly. He visibly was shaken. He started speaking: "I've just driven here from Portland. I've never done anything like this before! God spoke to me that I was to come to this church and present the speaker with a sword!" . . . although he didn't have a sword. (GOD'SIDENCE!) (No one knew about all the sword stuff that was happening, except a few close friends in my home area who were praying for Cornwall.) The Holy Spirit certainly had another thing planned for the meeting that evening. The pastor of that church, as well as the congregation, all believed this was God's doing. The man said he thought he was supposed to "dub me," or in other words, "knight me." So I followed instructions and got down on my knees while this man took an imaginary sword and knighted me. When I stood to my feet, the man said, "Uh, here!" and presented me with an imaginary sword. (GOD'SIDENCE!)

I did not fail to take note of what the Lord just had done. He was answering my questions concerning authority or a right to be in or have something to do with Cornwall.

The sword gifts kept coming . . . pins, earrings, shirts, souvenirs, pictures, and prophetic words. It seemed endless. (GOD'SIDENCES!)

A Flaming Sword

Yet another service, where I was preaching, was interrupted. This time my mother was with me. About 40 minutes into the sermon, a man sitting about midway to the back jumped up and tried to speak. He had turned white and was shaking all over. Of course, we all wondered what was wrong with him. Finally, after several seconds, he began to speak, "Angels, angels! There are four giant angels, one standing on each corner around you and another one that is even bigger is standing behind you waving a flaming sword over your head!" (GOD'SIDENCE!)

These "sword" occurances continued to happen over a two-year period of time. After taking the first large team of 56 to Cornwall in 1994, everything having to do with swords just stopped.

The Real Thing

In the summer of 2003, while attending a conference meeting, I met two ministers for the first time. They each have ministries in the greater Seattle area. One of them asked if we could meet over some coffee and discuss some of the spiritual things that were going on with him and his family and their ministry. We met and both of us got so excited about the things of the Lord that we did not want to "shut up" but we had to because of the time. Later that week, he called and invited me to dinner at their home. When I arrived, I learned that the other minister I had met and his wife also would be joining us.

We sat around and talked after dinner and were having a wonderful time. Then one of them stated that he believed the Lord wanted them to pray and speak prophetically over me. He asked if that would be alright with me. Of course, they could if they liked; I would be blessed to have them pray over me. They were all prophetic. Then the minister who had joined us that night said, "I believe the Lord has instructed me to pray specifically, and it will require that you get on your knees. Is that alright with you?" He asked. I told him, "Yes," that it was fine with me. Instantly I had an excitement in my spirit. Then they all gathered around me to pray. I looked up as he reached for a real sword with which he knighted me! Then they presented the sword to me. (GOD'SIDENCE!) It was a reenactment of what was done eight years earlier in the spirit (the imaginary sword). I am still in awe of what the Lord has done and is doing.

That sword is really something! It is almost as tall as I am and it is so heavy I hardly can lift it, **except when the Lord supernaturally gives to me added strength.**

A Woman With a Sword

This last October (2003) we went again on mission to Cornwall, a team of 19 people. The sword went with us, as did banners that were made with exact instructions from the Lord with detailing that was incredible! During one of our evening gatherings in our hotel, a lady and her husband attended who brought a journal of all the things the Lord had been showing them concerning Cornwall. They asked if they could share it with us. Of course, we said, "Yes," because we wanted to know everything that was going on in Cornwall; we have a lot of years invested. The lady began to read from her journal and after about five minutes, she read, "Then God gave me a vision and I saw a woman in white standing at the sea down around the west area with one foot in the water and one on the land. In her hand was a sword and she held it high!" (GOD'SIDENCE!) Our whole team jumped. Just that very day we had gone to the "west gate" down by the sea and I had raised the sword! I also happened to be wearing white. (GOD'SIDENCE!) No, they had not seen us nor had they heard anything. Besides, it already had been recorded in the journal for quite some time.

Concerning the banners we took to Cornwall, a very dear friend of mine, Judy Miller, had been instructed by the Lord to make them. Every item on those banners was prophetic. She was told to make one for the north, east, west and south gates of Cornwall. I knew she was making banners but had no idea they were for the gates until after we arrived in Cornwall. Those gates represent truth, righteousness, holiness, and peace and love.

A Woman With a Sword

Prior to leaving Seattle, the pastor and members of our fellowship gathered around me to pray for the team that was going to Cornwall. (Remember the team is made up of people from many different states in the United States.) One of the men there who is very gifted prophetically began praying, and in the middle of his prayer he started prophesying. "The Lord calls Cornwall married. Married to Jesus. She is His betrothed." I was very excited because I could share that "word" with the people of Cornwall.

The banner that the Lord had Judy make for the west gate (which had Holiness written on it) was made from the white satin material used to make her wedding dress! (GOD'SIDENCE!) In light of the words "betrothed and married" for Cornwall, the fact that the material used for the Holiness banner was for a bridal dress is significant prophetically.

I hardly can sit still while I am writing this. Just thinking about it makes me excited all over again!

Divine Appointments

In 1990 the Lord spoke to my heart concerning going to the four corners or four gates (whichever you prefer to call them). I like gates because the word signifies a doorway of entrance or exit. Whether corners or gates, it speaks of going to the north, east, west and south of the world, in that order.

At one point, some months earlier in the summer of 1989, the Lord had given a team of intercessors a word of knowledge concerning Israel being the center of the world. (GOD'SIDENCE!) They called me and excitedly told me that God had given me a key concerning the four gates (directions or corners). (GOD'SIDENCE!)

My secretary, Teresa, and I both prayed for the Lord to tell us where these four places were. We were willing to go if we knew where to go.

One day Teresa and I were driving across the state to an Aglow meeting, where I would be the guest speaker. As I drove, I must have been thinking about the four gates (corners or directions) and where they might be, because suddenly I spoke to her these words: "You know, honey, we might have to go to Israel before God will tell us where these four places are." (GOD'SIDENCE!) That was a bit strange and we just let the thought go. We spoke to no one of the matter. Two days later we received a call from pastors in Oregon who said these words: "Glorian? God has a word for you. He said to tell you that you must go to Israel and ask Him where the four corners of the world are located." (GOD'SIDENCE!) There were more instructions, as well, but that is for another volume.

Divine Appointments

After hanging up the telephone, Teresa and I both, as the saying goes, were climbing up the walls with excitement. We recognized that what was spoken in the car actually had been God giving instructions, and He just had confirmed it. (GOD'SIDENCE!)

We set about praying as to the timing for the trip to Israel. We received two more telephone calls from different people. One asked where I was going next and I replied Israel. She wanted to know when but I only could tell her that I did not know yet. She made this statement, "Oh, then you must be going late in December to that big conference." (GOD'SIDENCE!) I told her I did not know when we were leaving, but I did register the fact that it was the first date that had come to us in any fashion. The next call was from a Christian attorney (who today pastors a Jewish-Christian Fellowship with her husband). She spoke these exact words. "Glorian, where are you going next?" This was very strange because I barely knew this woman. I told her that I was going to Israel. She continued, "Well, you are supposed to go to Jerusalem and you are to stay in a prayer house that is on the top of the Mount of Olives. You are supposed to be on the roof of that house between the hours of three a.m. and six a.m., and God is going to give you the information you have come seeking! You must be completed with this assignment by the first day of spring!" (GOD'SIDENCE!) I told her that I was staying in that house. (GOD'SIDENCE!) She was astounded. "How do you know Tom Hess?" Through a divine appointment, the Lord had arranged for me to meet Tom just a short while previously. (GOD'SIDENCE!)

At that point in time we had two dates that had come, late in December and the first day of spring. That was a three-month span of time, give or take a few days. God was narrowing it down.

God'sidences (God's Intervention Today)

The last week of November, 1990, came and I was getting a bit concerned about our time to go. If it was to be late December, then we had only a month left before departure, and we had no tickets nor preparations done. As I spoke with the Lord that day, I told Him, "Lord, if You do not give me a specific departure date soon, then I am going to presume that we can choose the dates anytime within that three-month time frame" (which in some cases would be fine).

Knowing that Teresa and her family had prayer time together each evening, I asked her if she would ask them to pray for a specific departure date for us. That same evening I was visiting with friends of mine in a nearby community. I just had finished telling them the whole story about going to Israel and our struggle for a specific departure date. In the midst of our conversation their 17-year-old son came in the door from having been at basketball practice. Without any explanation, my friend, Shari looked up at him and said, "Tyson, when do you think Glo ought to go to Israel?" He looked toward the ceiling, tapped his chin, and then looked directly at me with pointed finger and said, "January 17th!" Then he just walked away. (GOD'SIDENCE!) You and I both know that was not normal! Most teenagers (or anyone else for that matter) would say something such as, "Oh, why are you going to Israel?" Or "I don't know."

Later in the evening, after my return home, I telephoned Teresa to tell her what had happened. Before I had a chance to explain, she said, "Oh, Glo, tonight when I asked the family about praying for a specific departure date, Marny (her 13-year-old daughter) looked down at the floor and then up at me and said, 'Well Mom the number 17 comes to me.'" (GOD'SIDENCE!) Again, not the norm!

Divine Appointments

Can you imagine our excitement? We had our answer! We were departing for Israel on January 17, 1991. There was no doubt in either of us. We knew we had heard from God!

Everything was so exciting as pastors in various cities began to speak over us and prophesy. The words given to us would be the same from all the pastors, without knowledge of the others. (GOD'SIDENCE!)

Then January 17th rolled around. We were scurrying about that morning taking care of last minute details before driving to the airport, which was about 100 miles away. The telephone rang and it was our travel agent calling to tell me our flights had been canceled. "What?" I said. She went on to say, "Haven't you heard? There is a war going on!" No, I had not heard! "Nanda, listen to me. You must put us on another flight then." She said it would be impossible because of the terrorism everywhere. "Nanda! I don't care where you send us, just get us out of here." She called a few minutes later and said we had flights, but within a short time afterward, she called back and those flights, too, had been canceled.

Once again I addressed her very sternly: "Nanda, **GOD** said for us to depart today and depart we will! Put us on a flight to Cairo, or Istanbul, or Romania, or wherever—we'll walk in if we have to! It is imperative that we leave today! We are not dealing with just anyone here, we are dealing with God, Maker and Ruler of the whole world!"

About 20 minutes went by and she called again. "Alright, I have you booked on the last remaining flight into Israel on the Israeli Airline. [GOD'SIDENCE!] Don't ask me how I did it, you don't want to know. There is one problem, though, you must have $840 more in my hand within the next two hours." With heart pounding, I replied, "Book it!" and then hung up the telephone. (To this date I do not know how she did it. All I knew was that God was having His way!)

God'sidences (God's Intervention Today)

We did not have $840. All we had was the food money on which we would need to survive while we were overseas. "Okay, Lord, You said depart today and we need more money." In the next half an hour to 40 minutes $840 came into my hands! (GOD'SIDENCE!) It came in segments, but it came! God was directing everything. He had me ask three people for money, which totaled $475. (This was the only time the Lord ever has directed me to ask for money.) Immediately after that, people just started calling and telling me they had money they wanted to give to us for our trip, etc. Others came to the door unannounced saying they wanted to give. It was truly miraculous.

There were also those who called and told us we were not supposed to go because there was a war going on and it would be too dangerous. I had to deal with each opposition, telling them that I did not believe God had changed His mind just because there was now a war.

Don't you, Dear Reader, think God knew there was going to be a war and that is why He was so specific about the departure date? (GOD'SIDENCE!) In other words, **GOD DOES NOT CHANGE HIS MIND JUST BECAUSE THE CIRCUMSTANCES MAY CHANGE!** I believe the Lord had purpose in placing us in Israel at that exact time in history.

It was already quite late at night when we made it to Jerusalem. Almost as soon as we arrived, the sirens began signaling that there was a missile on the way and that everyone was to get into a sealed room.

At 3:00 a.m., though the assignment was unusual, the Lord gave me the strength and courage to be obedient and leave the sealed room and go to the roof during the first night of our arrival. He, indeed, gave me the locations of the four places He wanted to send us, on a world scale, within the three hours of allotted time upon that roof. (GOD'SIDENCE!)

Divine Appointments

God had a plan! It was like killing two birds with one stone, because we remained throughout the war, praying and ministering daily. (GOD'SIDENCE!)

Steps Ordered by God

Having been on several overseas assignments, I began to pray for contacts so I could preach in three nations, Singapore, England, and Germany. It was around the time I would be going to Jakarta on a mission from God. Jakarta, Indonesia, is where the Lord sent me, representing the east gate of the world.

I still had about a month and a half before the mission. I was at home and the telephone rang. It was my mother and she said that she and my dad had just put an airplane ticket in the mail for me to go and attend a large international conference in Los Angeles, California. She continued to tell me that she had taken care of everything: the registration, the hotel and money for food. I told her didn't think I could go because I was tired and had been running a fever since getting home from a trip a week or so prior. She responded with, "Well, I know we heard from God and are supposed to send you! But if you really can't go then send the ticket, etc., back to us." As I hung up the phone, I remember saying, "Lord, what do they think they're doing anyway, they can't afford to send me anywhere." The light went on because that was correct. They could not afford to send me anywhere, and they would not have done it unless they believed it had been God's instruction. (GOD'SIDENCE!) I called them back and told them I would go.

I still was not feeling well when leaving for the conference. Upon arrival I checked into the hotel and then went to bed. The next morning, bright and early, I joined with all the others waiting for the doors of the conference center to be opened.

The line was about four abreast as we waited. I turned to the young lady standing next to me and asked her what her name was. She answered as she turned around to face me. "Snowda. Snowda Quak!" I looked at her name badge and it said she was from Singapore. I started laughing and told her that I would soon be in Singapore. She then started tapping a man in front of her, as she said, "Pastor? Pastor?" That man stuck his hand in his pocket as he was turning around. He pulled out a business card and handed it to me as he said, "You are coming to Singapore? Then you must come and preach in my church." (GOD'SIDENCE!) The doors opened and the line started moving. Before I even could say anything, he had disappeared into the crowd. I never saw him again during that conference.

That man knew nothing! He did not know who I was or what I did. He did not know I was a preacher! So I was witnessing the power of God to intervene on my behalf. (GOD'SIDENCE!)

The next morning of the conference as I was leaving my hotel room, there was a lady leaving her room at the same time, which was down the hall. She looked up and saw me, then came darting toward me. "You're here! Last night the Lord awakened me and as I began to pray He put your face before me! He told me I must give you my cottage!" "What? Where is it?" I asked. "In Cornwall, England." (GOD'SIDENCE!) I was laughing and crying at the same time. I was sure that meant that the Lord was giving me contacts to preach and minister there. Little did I know what His plans were, though! He had something much more in mind. (That's what led me to Cornwall!)

The third day of the conference the Lord caused me to meet a German lady who invited me to go on a trip with her to Germany to minister to her family. (GOD'SIDENCE!) Although that was not exactly what I had in mind, I realized that **it was God showing me His abilities to orchestrate our lives.**

God'sidences (God's Intervention Today)

(GOD'SIDENCE) Nothing ever came about with that precious lady but I now have ministered in Germany and return often.

On the Way to Jakarta

When I got home from the conference in Los Angeles, I sat down and penned a letter to the young pastor who had invited me to speak in his church. I never heard from him in return, so I decided that I would call him when I arrived in Singapore.

This would be the first overseas trip that I took where I did not have all the airline tickets that I would need to accomplish the task the Lord set before me. It was one of those times when just the smallest tug causes you to stop what you are doing. I had gone to the travel agency to pay for and pick up my tickets. While standing there, I had the impression that I should wait to purchase the ticket that would take me from Singapore to Jakarta and back to Singapore. (GOD'SIDENCE!) It was the Lord's way of answering my plea for extra cash so I actually could help someone on foreign soil meet their needs.

Arriving in Singapore, I checked into the YMCA. Once settled in my room, I called the pastor (Stephen Goh) who had invited me to speak. He answered the telephone and I proceeded to tell him who I was. He said, "I have nothing for you. I do not know why I gave you my card! I am really sorry." I told him that was fine, that it was not a big deal. We said our "good-byes" and hung up.

The next order of business was finding out if there was a travel agency nearby. The front desk gave me directions to one pretty close. I walked there in a short time. The owner happened to be a Christian man and God gave me favor with him. Buying the ticket in Singapore, versus the United States, saved me almost $500. (GOD'SIDENCE!) I was so excited! God had arranged for me to have extra money to help meet some needs of the people. I love giving money away, from Jesus! It often completely changes a life!

It was Saturday and my main business was done. That meant I could eat and then get to bed right away. It was mid-afternoon. I figured that if I could get to bed in an hour or so, I would be well rested by morning, after my long journey.

Leaving the travel office I was very pleased. As I was walking back to the YMCA, I happened to look inside the windows of a large mall. I saw the words printed over a shop that said, "TRUMPET PRAISE." I turned and went inside. I asked the man behind the counter if this was a Christian place? He guardedly answered with, "We sell Christian books and tapes." I then asked if he was a Christian. His reply was evasive. He asked, "Are you a Christian?" I told him I was and he burst into a smile and said, "Yes, I am a Christian!" Before I knew what I was doing, I began scolding the man. "Young man, don't you ever do that again! If you are ashamed of Jesus before man, then He'll be ashamed of you before the Father!" He was repentant. Then he asked me to come the following morning and preach in his church. (GOD'SIDENCE!) He pastored a good-sized congregation as well as traveled internationally as an evangelist. Seems he had been filling in at the shop for someone else who needed help for a couple of hours. (GOD'SIDENCE!)

Again I saw the hand of God move on my behalf. I thought to myself, "So the meeting with the pastor in California didn't work out, oh well." I was still in awe of the way things were happening.

I was back in my room at the YMCA for only a short time when the telephone rang. It was Stephen, the young pastor whom I had met in California. He said, "O.K. we have something for you. We will come and get you in the morning and you will minister in our church." I had to explain that I was sorry but was no longer available for the next morning. Stephen was shocked when he heard that I was going to be preaching in the other church. "How do you know them?" He asked. I explained and then we made arrangements for special meetings at which he wanted me to preach. (GOD'SIDENCE!)

At one point during my stay in Singapore (after I had completed my mission in Jakarta), Stephen called me and asked if he could come and pick me up because he and the people of his fellowship had a surprise for me. When we arrived at the church, the congregation was waiting for me. They went on to explain that they had stayed up all night at the church and prayed, and that the Lord had instructed them that their church was to be my Asian office . . . that the Lord had told them to take care of any need that I may have when it concerned Asia. (GOD'SIDENCE!) They still do!

By the time I actually left Singapore, Stephen and his wife, Angela, and I had become fast friends. As the years have gone by, Stephen has become as a son to me. (GOD'SIDENCE!) **Oh, taste and see that the Lord is good!**

My main mission in Asia during that time was to go to Jakarta, the east gate of the world, to carry out the prophetic assignment the Lord had given to me. As I've explained already, prior to going there I spent a short time in Singapore. When the churches found out that I was going to Jakarta, they asked if I had gotten a new passport since my time in Israel? I told them, "No." They then informed me that I had better not attempt to get into Jakarta until I got a new one. They said it could be dangerous for me. Besides, "They will not let you into the country!" they assured me.

For just a few moments I was stunned. What about all the money already used just getting that far? Why didn't I know that about the passport? My mind was racing. Then the peace of God flooded my soul. (GOD'SIDENCE!) I told them not to worry, if God already had performed so many miracles, signs, and wonders getting me this far, then I needn't worry about it. I was going to board that airplane and God would do the rest.

Of course, you know that all the way to Jakarta I was praying, "Oh, God, please blind their eyes. You did it for the Bible smugglers and I know you can do it for me!"

Upon arrival, of course, everyone must go through customs. I stood in a long line waiting my turn, still praying. When it came my turn I was holding my breath. The officer took my passport and started to look through it, one page at a time. Just before he got to the page which had the Israeli stamp on it, another officer behind him asked a question, and the one holding my passport turned to the next page right past the one with the stamp of Israel. (GOD'SIDENCE!) God had blinded their eyes!

I often wonder why I allow myself to ever get stressed over anything?

Needless to say, the church in Singapore was amazed that I had gotten into Jakarta. When God intervenes, all things become possible. My faith was increased, as was the faith of the brothers and sisters at Zion Christian Center.

A Heart for Poland

For months I had been praying for contacts in Europe (I had not been yet). One day the telephone rang and it was a minister that I knew, although not well. She said that the Lord had instructed her and her husband to take a team to Poland. (GOD'SIDENCE!) She also said that neither of them wanted to take a team and had told the Lord so. His reply to them was to, "Call Glo Bonnette and she will help you do this." They went on to give me the dates.

At that moment I had heard nothing from the Lord, and so I declined. "I'm really sorry but I already have engagements during that time." She said, "Glo, you should really pray about this!" The very second I hung up the telephone receiver, the Lord began dealing with me. "I thought you were praying for contacts in Europe!" He said. (GOD'SIDENCE!) "Oh, God, what have I done?" I called the couple back and told them I would cancel all my speaking engagements and go with them. I next asked them how much the trip was going to cost. They told me $1,300.

Within a very short time the telephone rang, and it was a missionary friend who asked me, "Glo, where are you going next?" I told her I just had gotten an invitation into Poland. She immediately said, "Oh, then put me down for $500." Shortly after that, my husband called and informed me that the Z28 had just sold and, after he took what he needed, there was $800.00 left for me.

Wow! Within one hour's time from the invitation, I had $1,300. (GOD'SIDENCE) I figured God really wanted me to go.

God'sidences (God's Intervention Today)

(Next the Lord gave me a 66-passenger bus with only 20,000 original miles on it. That's another story but I'm not going to record it in this book.)

The trip was wonderful and all eight of us on the team ministered in a couple of churches and a Bible School. At one point in the trip, though, all eight of us got on a train and went for a ten-hour trip to Warsaw, the capital of Poland, to retrieve one of our guitars that the airline had misplaced. (GOD'SIDENCE!)

While in Warsaw, we first went to the airport and then back to the train station. We looked at every shop in that underground area, as well as sang some songs. Then we decided to walk to the cultural tower and climb to the top.

At the top of the building we began to pray and prophesy over the city and the nation. The Lord caused the most amazing overwhelming love for Poland and that great city to be set in my heart during that time. I walked away from the group weeping and asking the Lord to give me contacts in that great city that I might minister to the people—to my brothers and sisters in Christ!

The time arrived when I was to take a team to Archangel, USSR. There were three of us going, two women and one man. We applied for visas but they never came. We already had purchased our non-refundable airline tickets that would take us to Warsaw, where we would change planes. We were sure that we were to leave on the appointed date. We really were praying, "God help us!"

The visas still had not come and we had only two days before departure. I did not know what we were going to do. I did not know a soul in Warsaw and did not know how we ever would get things arranged to get across the border into Russia (the USSR). Then the Lord reminded me that He was God of the impossible. **(Oh, how quickly we sometimes can forget!)**

A Heart for Poland

Right down to the wire, with less than 15 hours to departure, I received a telephone call from a lady whom I knew. As we visited, I told her of our dilemma. She responded with, "I met a preacher who I think has been to Poland and Russia. He is from Everett or somewhere in that area. His ministry is called 'Storehouse Ministries' and his name is Ed Allen." (GOD'SIDENCE!)

After hanging up from our conversation, I called information and found a number for the Storehouse ministry. I called and the person on the other end informed me that Ed was not available because he was in Florida. She asked me what I needed and I briefly told her. I also left my name and telephone number. I hung up disappointed. A short while later, though, Ed himself called me. (GOD'SIDENCE!) Needless to say, I was very shocked and pleased to hear from him. He went on to inform me that he only knew one man in Warsaw, a pastor. He said he did not know if the man were still alive because he had heart problems. He gave me the name of the pastor, the church name, the address, and his telephone number.

The Hotel Clerk

Upon arrival in Warsaw, we went directly to a hotel. Registering was not going to be easy because we did not understand one word of the language. When the desk clerk heard us speaking English, she raised her hand and said, "Moment." She left the room and another lady came out to help us. She spoke very good English, and I felt blessed that the hotel we had chosen employed her. When we finished checking in, I told the young lady that we needed one more thing from her if that were possible. "What do you need?" She asked. "We need to make a telephone call. Can you help us?" I inquired. "Let me see your number," she said. I opened my name and address book to the proper page and pointed to it. She very loudly spoke, "Bolec Dawidow! This is my pastor! This is my church!" (GOD'SIDENCE!) She was so excited that she hardly could contain herself. "You are Christians! This is my first day to work here, and I prayed that God would send me some Christians!" (GOD'SIDENCE!) You well can imagine our excitement, too! She made the telephone call and then handed me the receiver.

The Pastor

I spoke with the pastor, telling him we were on assignment from the Lord, and we needed help getting papers filled out at the Russian Embassy, and that we needed a place to stay because we did not have enough money to stay in the hotel for long. He replied that he was sorry but he could not help us. He said they were having a big conference, and all the homes of the congregation were full, and that he had no time to go to the embassy. He hung up.

That night the lady with me (Shari Ziegler) and I prayed and danced in our room. We figured that was the best thing we could do. Early the next morning the telephone rang, awakening us. It was the pastor saying, "O.K. I help you! My wife, she beat me up in the night." I later learned that she had awoken him by hitting him on the chest while urgently saying, "Bolec, Bolec! You must help them! It is God!" (GOD'SIDENCE!)

They came and picked us up and took us to someone's flat. It was a large flat with two bedrooms. The owner of the flat said we could come, and she would go and stay with her mother until we no longer had need of it. (GOD'SIDENCE!) We were ten days getting visas into the USSR.

While waiting, Sunday rolled around and, of course, we went to pastor Bolec's church. They had a guest speaker that Sunday from Scotland. It was wonderful to be able to hear the message in English. The service was quite lengthy but we didn't mind. When they had finished, pastor Bolec stood up and announced in his deep and very expressive voice, "And now, we

God'sidences (God's Intervention Today)

have another guest speaker, Rev. Glo Bonnette!" What a surprise! I asked him, "What do you want me to speak about?" With a large expression he said, "Whatever is on your heart, of course!"

I don't remember what I spoke during that time, but I was about 20 minutes into the service when all of a sudden it dawned upon me that I was preaching in the great city of Warsaw! (GOD'SIDENCE!) God had arranged a contact for me, making it possible for me to minister in the city over which I had prayed months earlier while standing in the top of the tower of culture in the city center.

To top it off, the contact that the Lord arranged, Pastor Bolec Dawidow, was the Apostle who started an entire denomination that is throughout Poland. He was a great man of faith. I came to love him dearly, as a Papa. It was thanks to God and Bolec that today I have ministered all over Poland. (GOD'SIDENCE!) Imagine the Lord introducing me to the one man who could open the doors for me.

What an all powerful and mighty God we serve!

Angels Everywhere

In 1989, the Lord spoke to me. "Make reservations for Singapore, Japan, and Korea." So I inquired of the Lord and asked Him what was I to do. His instructions to me were: "Walk the land and pray what I tell you to pray, and understand I have set up divine appointments for you." I did not know what would happen on that trip but my desire was to be obedient to my Lord Jesus Christ, knowing that He is trustworthy!

A few weeks later I received a check in the mail from a couple in Panama. I did not know them. I still do not know them. They stated in a letter that the Lord had instructed them to send me money and to tell me it was for a trip. (GOD'SIDENCE!) That check arriving was the confirmation that I needed at that time to know God really was sending me.

I knew Singapore was hot and humid but I did not have extra money to go out and buy a new wardrobe, so I packed what I owned. It was more important for me to go than to fuss with clothing. The only problem was that my clothes were suitable only for the pacific northwestern part of the United States. At that time I did not even own a pair of flat shoes, of any kind! I was a high-heel girl!

Arriving in Asia, I began walking and praying in my high heels. I dared not spend the money on anything extra. My funds were very limited, and I wanted to be a good steward of the money the Lord had given to me.

As the days went by, my feet were pretty swollen and painful. One day as I was walking, a Chinese woman approached

God'sidences (God's Intervention Today)

me with her hand held in a position on my chest to stop me. I asked her what she wanted but she did not answer me. Instead, she bent down and tugged at my ankle so that I would raise my foot off the pavement. When I raised it she removed my high heel, then she took the shoe off her foot and placed it on mine. She repeated the process with the other foot. Then she picked up both of my heels and handed them to me and walked off barefoot on the hot pavement. (GOD'SIDENCE!)

She never did say one single word.

Those shoes were brand new. The soles were not even dirty. They were made of soft leather with elastic around the top and they had rubber corrugated soles. THEY JUST FIT ME! (GOD'SIDENCE!)

I believe she was an angel sent by God to provide for my need.

The next provision came after the Lord sent me to two more nations to which I did not know I was going, Malaysia and Indonesia. I was concerned because of my limited funds. As I would seek the Lord, He always would say, "Trust Me!"

With only a few days left before I was to fly to Japan, I was concerned that I did not have enough money left to pay for the hotel and to continue my trip. Still I was walking and praying until time to leave.

Again I was stopped on the street. This time it was a man. As he stood in front of me, he put his hand into his suit breast pocket and pulled out an envelope, which he then handed to me. He, too, walked away without having said one word.

I opened the envelope and it was filled with money. (GOD'SIDENCE!) More money than I had already spent! **I believe he was an angel sent by God to provide for my need, once again.**

Another time the Lord gave me instructions that included taking a team to Corpus Christi, Texas, to do a very unusual prophetic assignment. It was not the normal kind of thing to do. I was told, "Glo, take a stick and write upon it CORPUS CHRISTI BELONGS TO JESUS!" When I had finished doing that, the Lord said, "Now, deliver it to the highest city official in Corpus Christi, Texas."

Once we were in Corpus Christi, the task was not unnoticed because there were government dignitaries meeting there that day in the offices of the person to who we were to give the stick. As you can well imagine, we were trying our best to stay calm and not look as if we were fools.

When the task was completed, all seven of us got on the elevator and went down to the lobby on the first floor. As the elevator doors opened, there was an oriental man standing there dressed in a suit. He was so shining that he appeared as though he had been oiled. He was holding up both of his thumbs and said, **"It's a job well done!"** (GOD'SIDENCE!) He stepped onto the elevator and then **"poof"— he vanished before our eyes!** We were stunned, realizing we just had seen an angel. (No, the elevator doors had not closed!)

The most amazing part was that God sent him to tell us that He was pleased with how we carried out the task. (GOD'SIDENCE!)

Another time Teresa and I were driving across Kansas on a Sunday afternoon, headed for the west coast, when we heard this horrible noise.

I looked in the rear view mirror and saw rubber flying everywhere! I thought the tires were losing their tread. I pulled the car over to the shoulder and shut it off. Both of us looked at the tires and saw that they were fine. So then we raised the hood and rubber was everywhere. Being as we just had gotten the car out of the shop that morning, after seven previous breakdowns, I was ready for a good cry. I was frustrated and

God'sidences (God's Intervention Today)

did not know what to do. All of a sudden, a man said, "Get into your car and go to the next exit. You still have enough power to get there." Both of us turned and saw this man walking from his car toward us. (How did he get there? He was not there when we pulled off the road and he did not pass us. There was nothing coming from the other direction either.) He was only half way when he had begun speaking. Again he spoke, forcefully. "I said get in your car. The problem is your fan belt, your_____ belt and etc." I started arguing with the man. "But, but sir . . . ." By the time he had reached us, he let down the hood of my car and sternly said, "Get into your car and go to the next exit. I'll be right behind you."

We watched him go back to his car and get in. I started the engine and pulled out real slow (I was afraid). As we passed him and his car, I was watching through the rear view mirror to make sure he followed us, as he said he would. Teresa was turned toward the back and was watching him through the back window. He pulled his big green car out onto the highway and then **"poof," the driver and the car vanished!** (GOD'SIDENCE!)

Once again the Lord had sent an angel in our time of need!

In Berlin one time, there were three of us together, and we just had gotten off a train and needed to change trains. It was a time when all the tracks were being switched and repaired and there was mass confusion everywhere. We looked around but were having a difficult time with literally hundreds of people shoving us. We knew we only had a few minutes to find the right train. Suddenly a man walked up and took my two bags and said, "Follow me!" The man on our team started to get upset with the man because he thought the man was stealing my bags. All I could say was, "Be quiet and follow him."

Angels Everywhere

That man led us to a train and then set my bags down right at the door and then walked away saying not one more word. (GOD'SIDENCE!)

Once again God came to the rescue by sending us an angel!

There is no other explanation because that man did not ask us where we were going, and we surely did not tell him. We were scrambling just to keep up with him; after all he had my bags. If he had not gone so fast we would have missed our train.

(GOD'SIDENCE!)

Remember the Bible says in Hebrew 13:2: "Do not forget to entertain strangers, for by doing so some have unwittingly entertained angels." (*NKJ*)

Let me paraphrase the same Scripture. "Do not neglect to show hospitality to strangers, for by this some have entertained angels without knowing it."

The New Century Version says: "Remember to welcome strangers into your homes. Some people have done this and have welcomed angels without knowing it."

Our Eyes Were Blinded

Once a team of us went to work with a young pastor in northern Poland who was going to do an outreach at a resort town on the Baltic Sea. The young people on the team were joining with the Polish brothers and sisters in doing some mime and skits, while we older saints stood back and watched. When the outreach was over we had some time to mull around, get a cold drink, and look at the tourist attractions. As I walked along, I saw many artists drawing portraits for a fee. There were several artists and they were all quite good but there was one young lady set up over by a hedge of greenery, tucked under a tree. Standing back and watching her, I noticed that no one bothered to stop and inquire about her ability. The Lord began dealing with my heart and causing compassion for her to grow. So I walked over to where she was and asked her how much? She replied 30,000 Zloty (around $3.75). I sat down and told her to draw a picture of me. While she was working the Lord continued to speak to me concerning the young lady. I asked her what her name was. "Malgosha," she replied and then in English said, "Margaret."

As the Lord continued to show me things about Margaret, the tears begin to well up in my eyes as I gingerly spoke. "Margaret, Jesus is telling me to tell you that He loves you!" She said, "Sh-h-h you must sit still. No talking." "I must talk because Jesus wants you to know He does love you!" Her eyes filled with tears and they began to run down her face until she had to stop and dry them and blow her nose. She then very politely asked me to be quiet.

Our Eyes Were Blinded

When the portrait almost was completed, one of the ministers and his daughter, who were both members of the team from the USA, walked over to where I was, and asked how much the picture was costing me. I told them the price, and he decided that he and his daughter would both have Margaret draw their pictures, too.

When all three portraits were completed and I started to get my money out, my brother asked if I had a couple of extra 50,000 Zloty bills? I said I thought so and dug through my wallet, producing three 50,000 Zloty bills. I handed all three bills, along with a copy of my testimony tract, to my brother to pass over to Margaret, as I was telling her, "Keep the change!" She stood as though stunned! "I cannot!" was her reply. I insisted, telling her: "It is from Jesus!" She stood looking shocked as we walked away.

Later that same day I got into my wallet to get some money to purchase something to eat and began to count my money. I was missing a large amount of money. We had gone to a Kantor (moneychanger) that very morning and I had exchanged US dollars for Polish Zloty's. I started to panic as I told everyone I was missing my money. The young pastor with us began to question me. "Glo, did you buy something? Did you have your money out where someone could see it?" "No, I did not. The only time I had it out or bought anything was for the three portraits!" He asked, "What size bills did you give to her?" I answered that I gave the artist three 50,000 Zloty bills. He then said are you sure they were 50's. At which point my brother interrupted, and said, "Glo handed the bills to me and they were 50,000 Zloty each."

Then I began to think perhaps the moneychanger had made a mistake and so we went back to see him. No mistake was made, his books all tallied up at the end of the day.

God'sidences (God's Intervention Today)

Everyone was upset and so finally the Lord shook me and I got some peace and perspective back. "Alright, everyone, listen. Let's just pray and ask the Lord to show us what happened to it." We prayed and let it go.

There is no good that can be done by stewing over something or as the saying goes, "Don't cry over spilled milk."

The Lord provided for the rest of our trip and so the "lost money" did not hinder us in the least.

Months later, I received a letter from Poland. It was from Margaret, the young artist. The letter was written in English. As I read it, her story unfolded in the most miraculous way. She told of her circumstances previous to our meeting, at which time she had been 18 years old. Here is her story.

Margaret was 17 when she got saved and became a Christian. When she accepted Jesus as her personal Savior, her Catholic family threw her out of their home. Margaret was living on the streets the best way she could but was not able to earn a living. The only thing she could do was draw. Everyday she would set up her easel and pray for someone to come and hire her. But there were only a few over a long time. She went on to relay that most people would go to the older more experienced artists and would not give her a chance. Finally, she had decided that Jesus did not love her. Yes, she could believe He loved others but not her!

"Then you came along," she said, "and you told me Jesus wanted me to know He did love me! Then when He gave me that million and one-half Zloty, I knew He really did!" (GOD'SIDENCE!)

Margaret went on to explain that it was enough money for her to move to a college town, rent an apartment, and pay in advance. Also she had enough money to buy materials and started a candle-making business, and pay tuition for school.

Our Eyes Were Blinded

Her business was good enough that it supported her thereafter.

The last time I had contact with Margaret, we met in Warsaw and spent a weekend together, where she presented me with the most beautiful candle you can imagine. It was white with gold flowers carved and painted gold along with the words, "To my only American friend."

Just think about the goodness of God. What a miraculous provision to show His daughter how much He did love her and cared about her circumstances.

Consider the Lord's faithfulness also concerning the money. He, indeed, answered our prayers and showed us what happened to it! (GOD'SIDENCE!) Our eyes must have been blinded because both my brother and I could have sworn it was 50,000 Zloty bills and not 500,000 Zloty bills. At that time, the money in Poland was about 8,000 Zloty to $1.00. Somewhere between $150 and $300 was an average monthly income at that time for those who were considered as having a good job . . . such as a scientist.

Prophetic in Number

In 1989, the Lord instructed me to take a team to the border of every state in the USA. We were instructed at every border to:
1. Blow a trumpet.
2. Repent for the sins He would show us.
3. Take Communion and then bury half of it (as a sign of His presence).
4. Prophesy to the leaders of that state.

The Lord gave us one year to complete that prophetic assignment. Of course, you know right away the kind of things that were hitting me. "Lord, what about money? What about people leaving their jobs for so long? What about people leaving their families for that long? How do we do this?" Obviously, the Lord was gracious and calmed me down.

As the weeks passed, the picture came into clearer view. We were to use a motor home. We could divide the task into four trips. He would bring those He desired to be a part of the team. He gave each member favor with his/her employer, as well as with his/her family members. He supplied our every need financially! (GOD'SIDENCES!)

As we headed out in the motor home, most of the team was somewhat upset because we were not always on a main highway. We were sometimes on small roads in ill repair. Ours was a directional "pathway," chosen by God during over 100 hours in prayer. They were upset because being on a pathway versus a highway causes motion sickness. Thereafter our trips were referred to as, "The pathway" of America. (GOD'SIDENCE!)

Our assignment was a prophetic one to the USA. We spoke to the leaders prophetically from each border, as well as at our nation's Capitol, the White House, the Supreme Court, and the Pentagon. The word was all about DIVINE GOVERNMENT, that chosen by God!

The number for government is 12.

The Lord brought together exactly 12 persons to carry out the assignment to the USA. (GOD'SIDENCE!)

It was exactly 12 years later, to the month, that 911 happened in New York. (GOD'SIDENCE!)

(Do you remember the struggle over the Presidency in the election year 2,000? President Bush won! He is God's chosen leader for this hour in history.) For the first time in the history of my life, I heard a President openly declare, "In God we trust!"

As I stood watching the television the morning of 911, the Lord instantly showed me the reenactment of the mission USA.

1. The towers were hit (the trumpet was blown).
2. The people began to repent (for their own sins and those of the nation.)
3. The people began to communicate with God (Communion).
4. The people began to prophesy, GOD BLESS AMERICA! (GOD'SIDENCE!)

This is the PATHWAY for the healing of America! (GOD'SIDENCE!)

1. HEAR! "Let he who has an ear hear what the Spirit is saying."
2. REPENT OF OUR SIN.

3. PRAY. "If my people who are called by my name will humble themselves and pray I will heal their nation."
4. PROPHESY. "God has the victory! God bless America!"

Prophetic Numbers Continued

In 1994, the Lord put together a team of 56 people that joined me in a mission. "Take 100 strong and change the complexion of Cornwall." Those were my instructions. Over the years, we repeatedly watched what happens concerning the number of people on the teams.

For instance: A shipping magnate built the Manor House (hotel) in which we stay in when we go to Cornwall. While there once, we found a book in the library, written about his life, and in that book it states that he owned many homes and ships. The strange thing was that he kept naming them the same 56 names. He repeatedly used 56 names and we were 56 people on that team! (GOD'SIDENCE!) By the time we left Cornwall, we had an understanding that each person on the team represented something that stood either for, or against the meaning of those names, in the spiritual realm. (GOD'SIDENCE!)

The next big team to go to Cornwall was in the year 2000. I was praying that the Lord would send me someone to help me put it together and to help me as leaders. A couple of days later, Kevin and Grace arrived on my doorstep with the words, "How would you like it if we helped you put together the next team for Cornwall?" (GOD'SIDENCE!) We had not previously discussed a thing concerning Cornwall. They were God's provision!

That team totaled 39 in number. One night during an evening gathering at our hotel, a gentleman stood and commented, "Did you say that there are 39 of you?" I confirmed it. He then said, "Today, when I saw you people on the streets, the Lord spoke to me and instructed me to pay close attention because this is the beginning of the visible healing for Cornwall!" He went on to say, with tears in his eyes, "Do you know the number of stripes Jesus took for our healing?"

Visible healing! For our healing He took 39 stripes and we were 39 members on the team. (GOD'SIDENCE!)

In Cornwall, within the last four years, a group has arisen called "The Cornwall Prayer Initiative" which has organized prayer groups all over the County! (GOD'SIDENCE!) God is doing a mighty work there and they are in revival! **Hearts being made alive unto God! Watch what comes out of Cornwall! God's people with a Holy Ghost fire in their sole!**

It has been 12 years, now, since the Lord showed me a vision about the revival fires starting from the Lands End area and traveling across all of the UK, the channel, and on into the mainland of Europe!

The last team we took to Cornwall was this past October, 2003, and we were 19 in number. During our mission, we used a lot of dance incorporated during our song times, as our music leader, Kevin, spoke on the restoration of the Tabernacle of David. We had a wonderful group of dancers with the team, and what a blessing they added to everything we did!

One day our bus driver decided to bring some books written about the various famous tourist sights in Cornwall. One book was written about the Merry Maidens' Circle.

Now mind you, I had no interest in seeing it again, having been there so many times before. After all, it was just a bunch of old stones in a circle in the middle of a cow pasture. (Bah —humbug!)

As we were enroute to somewhere, Grace, one of the leaders helping me, picked up one of the books that our bus driver had

Prophetic Numbers Continued

brought. "Glo, listen to this!" She proceeds to read the legend about the Merry Maidens' Circle. "It says they were 19 young maidens that were discovered making merry on the Sabbath so they were turned to stone!"

I just about came unglued with excitement. There it was again, a number of importance. There were 19 stones and 19 of us! (GOD'SIDENCE!) Instantly, revelation came and I realized the significance. **Those stones have stood for centuries as a prophetic sign against the Truth of God. We are supposed to make merry before God! And when we do not, our hearts become as stone (hard ground).**

We were preaching and teaching about the Tabernacle of David and the "making of merry" (the Lord wants us to have fun and to enjoy the life He has given to us). Do you think the timing wasn't perfect? (GOD'SIDENCE!) I get so amazed at what our Lord does.

Needless to say, we had the greatest time going to the Merry Maidens' Circle with singing and dancing and the waving of banners! It was one of my most favorite events throughout the trip. God's banner over us is love, and that day we proclaimed victory for the Church in Cornwall.

It is only by the grace of God that I have learned to "look and see" those things which are of prophetic significance. I do not try to set up something to be prophetic. I just follow my Jesus' instructions to the best of my ability as He gives me strength.

I never know what the numbers are going to be until it is time to take off on any mission. And I never know unless the Lord shows me that the number of people on the team is prophetic in itself. Also, please understand . . . it is most often **after the fact that understanding comes.**

Note: First comes the faith, then the obedience, and afterward the results.

Croatia

For those of you who do not recognize the name Croatia, it was formerly called Yugoslavia when under Communist rule. I had heard of Yugoslavia but, honestly, I only knew the general location. If you had asked me for the location, I would not have been able to tell you until just a few years ago.

It happened this way. The Lord sent me on an assignment, saying, "Deliver this word to My son in Monaco." I agreed. I thought I would need about $2,000 to cover expenses for me and for one other lady. I did not want to go alone for some reason.

In the meantime, I was asked to participate in an Ordination Service in Idaho. While driving there, I stopped in Hood River, Oregon, which was on my way and picked up a young lady whom I had led into the baptism of the Holy Spirit a few months earlier. She was Baptist and never had witnessed anything in a Pentecostal setting. After several hours on the road, we were getting hungry, so we stopped in a town and went into a grocery store to purchase some fruit and snacks. When I opened my purse to pay for the food, THERE WAS $2,000 IN MY PURSE! (GOD'SIDENCE!)

As you can imagine, I was jumping up and down with excitement. Which, of course, caused a scene, which, in turn, meant I had to explain to everyone the miracle that just had occurred! (GOD'SIDENCE!) That miracle provision just had produced a *double blessing*. Blessing number one, I got the money! Blessing number two, all the people in the store witnessed God's supernatural supply! The blessings seemed endless by the time we actually had gone to Monaco and returned to the USA once again.

The day arrived for my traveling companion, Pamela, and me to depart. It was March, 1997. We flew from Seattle to Milan, Italy. It was difficult making ourselves understood but I thanked the Lord that Pamela spoke some Spanish. (GOD'SIDENCE!)

We finally were able to purchase train tickets that would take us to Nice, France, which was only eight miles on the other side of Monaco.

We were on the train for about an hour or so, when God gave me the thought to pray for safety, which I immediately did! (GOD'SIDENCE!) Shortly thereafter, the train started slowing down. It was getting slower for quite a distance until finally it came to a stop. There was no platform on either side of the train. We could not see anything outside except countryside . . . no houses, no barns, nothing. Soon the conductor came through our car and said something to the passengers, where upon they all rose and started leaving the train.

Pamela and I had no idea what was wrong or what to do. We inquired the best we could, but we were instructed to, "Stay on the train!" The best we could understand is that our tickets were all the way to Nice, and if we left the train we would have to purchase new tickets. We did not have the money to do that, so we stayed on the train. After some time had gone by, another train pulled up beside ours and all the people boarded it and then it took off!

There we were, stranded without the foggiest notion of what to expect or do. We were praying when Pamela decided to check out the train. She went through car after car and found all deserted except one. At last she came upon a couple who were together. They also were English speaking. They came

God'sidences (God's Intervention Today)

back with Pamela and reported that to the best of their knowledge the brakes had failed on the train, and that a railroad crew would be coming to fix the brakes, and then we could be on our way once more.

God had intervened when He had said, "Pray for safety." I often wonder what would have happened if I had ignored His prompting.

The crew finally appeared about five hours after everyone else had dispersed. When the train started up once again, it went for about two hours and then pulled to a stop at a train station. Without any explanation, there we were—sitting alone for several more hours, just the four of us. We had the opportunity to talk to the young couple about Jesus. (GOD'SIDENCE!)

Finally, at about 10:00 p.m. we arrived in Nice. The young couple walked with us to a hotel where we all registered for the night. They would be leaving the next morning and so we said our "good-byes." We, too, would have to leave the following morning in search of a place more reasonable in price.

Morning came and we went down to talk to the man at the desk to inquire about other lodging, explaining that our money was limited. He went on to ask me what could we afford? I told him and he gave us the room at the price I had quoted. (GOD'SIDENCE!) God is so good! Richard, who was the Assistant Manager of the hotel, understood and spoke some English, certainly enough to carry on a good conversation. (GOD'SIDENCE!)

For some unknown reason Richard, decided to befriend us. (GOD'SIDENCE!) He told us which restaurants were near and reasonable and how to deal with a waiter who may try to cheat us, as well as give us all-around good advice.

Over the next few days, Richard told us his story. He was actually a news anchor (broadcaster) for a television station in

Croatia. Around that part of the world he was famous. He reported that his editorials concerning the war in Bosnia, etc., had become so controversial that there were death threats made upon his life, and he had to flee from the country. He was able to take refuge in France because he had dual citizenship due to the fact that his parents were from two different countries. One was Croatian and the other French.

One day Richard invited Pamela and me to come to his flat for a "Real Croatian meal!" The day arrived and we went to have dinner at Richard's. As soon as the meal was finished, he brought out a big box of pictures to show to us. They were of his wife and children and other family members. Then he brought out pictures of his beloved Croatia. He showed each photo of Croatia with pride, the love for his country was apparent.

As I looked at the photos of Croatia, I noticed that my heart went "thump-thump," (rather like skipping a couple of beats). Even though I saw the pictures, I was still a bit foggy as to the location of Croatia. I would need to see a map to get it fixed in my mind. Remember that was happening in March of 1997.

July of 1997 rolled around and I attended a conference in Yakima, Washington, hosted by Harold Eberle. During that conference, they had a speaker who had decided it would be good for everyone in attendance to pray for every nation of the world at the same time. They then proceeded to pass around a bucket with the names of the countries recorded on slips of paper. I stuck my hand in and pulled out "CROATIA." Instantly, my heart went "thump-thump, thump- thump." (GOD"SIDENCE!) I recognized the Lord's hand in it, so that was the beginning of prayer for Croatia.

A year or so later (1998) while attending a Sunday afternoon meeting at our fellowship, the Lord put before me a vision. He showed me His breath blowing into the center of the Adriatic

Sea. It blew so hard that it caused the waters to swell and spill over onto all the surrounding nations. I understood that the Lord was showing me a move of His Spirit that was on its way! When I went home I got out the globe and looked at all the nations surrounding that sea. Wow, the East Coast of the Adriatic was Croatia! "Thump-thump, thump- thump, thump-thump," went my heart! (GOD'SIDENCE!) That did it, from that point the Lord would compel me to pray for Croatia. I would sit on the floor holding the world globe between my legs and encircling it with my arms. The tears would run as the Lord placed that nation upon my heart, and not only that nation but also the surrounding nations in that area.

1999 rolled around and someone happened to show me an article written about the new target area in the world. Previously we'd had the 10/40 window and now they were calling this new one the 70/30 or something such as that. With it came a picture of the targeted area. It included Croatia and all the surrounding nations. (GOD'SIDENCE!) My heart really went "thump-thump, thump- thump, thump-thump, thump-thump."

The next year 2000 rolled around, and I was staying with a friend in eastern Oregon while ministering in that area. I asked her if I could use her computer to check my e-mail. She said, "Yes," and so I set about pulling it up on the Internet. When my box appeared, there was an e-mail from someone I did not know. I clicked on it and there it was:

> Dear Rev. Glorian Bonnette,
>
> My name is Kay and I pastor a church in Split, Croatia. Would you be so kind as to come to Croatia and minister to our Church? (GOD'SIDENCE!)

Croatia

I sat in stunned silence as I realized the miracle I was seeing. As with all the countries to which the Lord has sent me, this one, too, was divinely arranged.

Of course, I responded with an e-mail accepting the invitation, with one stipulation; I could not come until the Lord provided the finances with instructions that it was the right time to go to Croatia. The time came about in October, 2002.

That mission was five years in the making! Which brings me to say, please be patient. Do not become weary in well doing. All things have their seasons.

I could continue with many more GOD'SIDENCES, but I believe this volume has come to its closing.

I pray that this book has encouraged you, and that you have grown in your belief that all things are possible with God . . . also **that you would dare to step out in obedience, and then just watch and see what the Lord will do.**

Be of good cheer for your Father in Heaven knows what you need, especially in order to be about His business as He wills.

> Matthew 6:19-21 (*NKJV*) "Do not lay up for yourselves treasures upon earth, where moth and rust destroy and where thieves break in and steal, but lay up for yourselves treasures in heaven, where neither moth nor rust destroys, and where thieves do not break in and steal. For where your treasure is, there your heart will be also."